Words
of Wisdom

BOOKS BY BILLY GRAHAM

The Challenge – Sermons from Madison Square Garden, 1969
 cloth $4.50

World Aflame
 cloth $3.50   paperback 75¢

Peace with God
 cloth $3.50   paperback 75¢

Secret of Happiness
 cloth $2.95   paperback 75¢

Billy Graham Answers Your Questions
  paperback 75¢

BOOKS ABOUT BILLY GRAHAM

"Billy Graham" by John Pollock
 cloth $2.50   paperback 95¢

"The Making of a Crusader" by Curtis Mitchell
 cloth $1.50

"The Quotable Billy Graham" by Cort Flint
 cloth $1.50

"Crusades – 20 Years with Billy Graham" by John Pollock
  paperback $1.95

THE BILLY GRAHAM EVANGELISTIC ASSOCIATION

Box 779 (1300 Harmon Place), Minneapolis, Minnesota 55440
Box 841 (414 Graham Avenue), Winnipeg 1, Manitoba, Canada
Shirley House, 27 Camden Road, London, N.W. 1, England
820 Caltex House, Sydney, New South Wales, Australia
Box 870, Auckland, New Zealand
Decision, 102 Avenue des Champs-Elysees, Paris 8, France
Entscheidung, Postfach 16309, 6 Frankfurt/M, Germany
Decimex, Apartado 10742, Mexico 1, D.F., Mexico
Casilla 5055, Buenos Aires, Argentina
20 Samon Cho, Shinjuku Ku, Tokyo, Japan

Words of Wisdom

from
Living
Psalms and
Proverbs

Paraphrased by
Kenneth N. Taylor

Compiled by
George M. Wilson

Special Crusade Edition
WORLD WIDE PUBLICATIONS
1313 Hennepin Avenue
Minneapolis, Minnesota 55403

PREFACE

In a way unmatched by any other literature, the book of Psalms draws us apart from the workaday life of man, brings us into the sanctuary and directs us into precious communion with God. The Hebrew word for Psalms is *tehillim*, which in a general way means poems of praise composed to be sung.

The book of Psalms really gives us a summary of both the Old and New Testaments. All the way through the book, and particularly in the Messianic psalms, we find the message of the Christ to come. Our risen Lord referred to the Psalms in His last message before ascending to His Father. "All things must be fulfilled," He said, "which were written . . . in the psalms concerning me." In Colossians 3:16 the Apostle Paul tells the believers to "Remember what Christ taught and let His words enrich your lives and make you wise; teach them to each other and sing them out in psalms and hymns and spiritual songs, singing to the Lord with thankful hearts."

While the Psalms are all divinely inspired, they were composed at different times for different occasions, and have been put together rather independently of each other. King David was probably the author of most of the Psalms. In 2 Samuel 23:1 he is referred to as the Psalmist of Israel. One psalm was a prayer of Moses. Other psalms were written by Asaph, for in

2 Chronicles 29:30 we are told to praise the Lord "with the words of David, and of Asaph." The Chronicler calls Asaph a seer or prophet.

David's genius is found in his poetry. His lyrics became the psalter for the early church of God. No other book, perhaps, is as helpful to a Christian's devotional life as is the book of Psalms.

The Psalms are divided into five sections, also called books. Each section concludes with "Amen" or "Hallelujah." The first section ends with Psalm 41; the second with Psalm 62; the third with Psalm 89; the fourth with Psalm 106. We have purposely not made these divisions in this devotional edition, but rather have paragraphed the Psalms for the convenience of the reader using them for inspiration in his daily devotions.

GEO. M. WILSON

FOREWORD

The late Senator Everett Dirksen of Illinois once told me that one could not help but draw great inspiration from the reading of the Psalms and the Proverbs. For many years I have made it a practice to read five Psalms and a chapter of the book of Proverbs each day, aside from my other Bible reading and study, and it has been a great blessing to me.

By reading five Psalms and one chapter of Proverbs daily, you will be able to read them through each month. The Psalms will tell you how to get along with God, and the Proverbs will tell you how to get along with your fellowman. In Deuteronomy 6:5 we read, "Thou shalt love the Lord thy God with all thine heart, and with all thy soul, and with all thy might." In Leviticus 19:18 we read, "Thou shalt not avenge, nor bear any grudge against the children of thy people, but thou shalt love thy neighbor as thyself: I am the Lord." Both of these great affirmations are underlined in the Psalms and Proverbs.

In this book you have a wonderful treat in store. May God bless you as you begin to live in its pages.

BILLY GRAHAM

Psalms for the First Day

1 Oh, the joys of those who do not follow evil men's advice, who do not hang around with sinners, scoffing at the things of God: ² But they delight in doing everything God wants them to, and day and night are always meditating on His laws and thinking about ways to follow Him more closely.

³ They are like trees along a river bank bearing luscious fruit each season without fail. Their leaves shall never wither, and all they do shall prosper.

⁴ But for sinners, what a different story! They blow away like chaff before the wind!

⁵ They are not safe on Judgment Day; they shall not stand among the godly.

⁶ For the Lord watches over all the plans and paths of godly men, but the paths of the godless lead to doom.

2 What fools the nations are to rage against the Lord! How strange that men should try to outwit God! ² For a summit conference of the nations has been called to plot against the Lord and His Messiah, Christ the King. ³ "Come, let us break His chains," they say, "and free ourselves from all this slavery to God."

4 But God in heaven merely laughs! He is amused by all their puny plans. 5 And then in fierce fury He rebukes them and fills them with fear.

6 For the Lord declares, "This is the King of My choice, and I have enthroned Him in Jerusalem, My holy city."

7 His chosen One replies, "I will reveal the everlasting purposes of God, for the Lord has said to Me, 'You are My Son. This is Your Coronation Day. Today I am giving You Your glory. 8 Only ask, and I will give You all the nations of the world. 9 Rule them with an iron rod; smash them like clay pots!' "

10 O kings and rulers of the earth, listen while there is time. 11 Serve the Lord with reverent fear; rejoice with trembling. 12 Fall down before His Son and kiss His feet before His anger is roused and you perish. I am warning you — His wrath will soon begin. But, oh, the joys of those who put their trust in Him!

A Psalm of David when he fled from his son Absalom
3 O Lord, so many are against me. So many seek to harm me. I have so many enemies. 2 So many say that God will never help me. 3 But Lord, You are my shield, my glory, and my only hope. You alone can lift my head, now bowed in shame.

4 I cried out to the Lord, and He heard me from His Temple in Jerusalem. 5 Then I lay down and slept in peace and woke up safely, for the Lord was watching over me. 6 And now, although ten thousand enemies surround me on every side, I am not afraid! 7 I will cry to Him, "Arise, O Lord! Save me, O my God!" And He will slap them in the face, insulting them and breaking off their teeth.

⁸ For salvation comes from God. What joys He gives to all His people.

4 O God, You have declared me perfect in Your eyes; You have always cared for me in my distress; now hear me as I call again. Have mercy on me. Hear my prayer.

² The Lord God asks, "Sons of men, will you forever turn My glory into shame by worshiping these silly idols, when every claim that's made for them is false?"

³ Mark this well: The Lord has set apart the redeemed for Himself. Therefore He will listen to me and answer when I call to Him. ⁴ Stand before the Lord in awe, and do not sin against Him. Lie quietly upon your bed in silent meditation. ⁵ Put your trust in the Lord, and offer Him pleasing sacrifices.

⁶ Many say that God will never help us. Prove them wrong, O Lord, by letting the light of Your face shine down upon us. ⁷ Yes, the gladness You have given me is far greater than their joys at harvest time as they gaze at their bountiful crops. ⁸ I will lie down in peace and sleep, for though I am alone, O Lord, You will keep me safely.

5 O Lord, hear me praying; listen to my plea, O God my King, for I will never pray to anyone but You.
³ Each morning I will look to You in Heaven and lay my requests before You, praying earnestly.

⁴ I know You get no pleasure from wickedness and cannot tolerate the slightest sin. ⁵ Therefore proud sinners will not survive Your searching gaze; for how You hate their evil deeds. ⁶ You will destroy them for their lies; how You abhor all murder and deception.

⁷ But as for me, I will come into Your Temple protected by Your mercy and Your love; I will worship You with deepest awe.

⁸ Lord, lead me as You promised me You would; otherwise my enemies will conquer me. Tell me clearly what to do, which way to turn. ⁹ For they cannot speak one truthful word. Their hearts are filled to the brim with wickedness. Their suggestions are full of the stench of sin and death. Their tongues are filled with flatteries to gain their wicked ends. ¹⁰ O God, hold them responsible. Catch them in their own traps; let them fall beneath the weight of their own transgressions, for they rebel against You.

¹¹ But make everyone rejoice who puts his trust in You. Keep them shouting for joy because You are defending them. Fill all who love You with Your happiness. ¹² For You bless the godly man, O Lord; You protect him with Your shield of love.

Proverbs for the First Day

1 These are the proverbs of King Solomon of Israel, David's son:

² He wrote them to teach his people how to live — how to act in every circumstance, ³ For he wanted them to be understanding, just and fair in everything they did. ⁴ "I want to make the simple-minded wise!" he said. "I want to warn young men about some problems they will face. ⁵, ⁶ I want those already wise to become the wiser and become leaders by exploring the depths of meaning in these nuggets of truth."

⁷, ⁸, ⁹ How does a man become wise? The first step is to trust and reverence the Lord!

Only fools refuse to be taught. Listen to your father and mother. What you learn from them will stand you in good stead; it will gain you many honors.

¹⁰ If young toughs tell you, "Come and join us" — turn your back on them! ¹¹ "We'll hide and rob and kill," they say; ¹² "Good or bad, we'll treat them all alike! ¹³ And the loot we'll get! All kinds of stuff! ¹⁴ Come on, throw in your lot with us; we'll split with you in equal shares."

[15] Don't do it, son! Stay far from men like that, [16] For crime is their way of life, and murder is their specialty. [17] When a bird sees a trap being set, it stays away, [18] But not these men; they trap themselves! They lay a booby trap for their own lives. [19] Such is the fate of all who live by violence and murder. They will die a violent death.

[20] Wisdom shouts in the streets for a hearing. [21] She calls out to the crowds along Main Street, and to the judges in their courts, and to everyone in all the land: [22] "You simpletons!" she cries, "how long will you go on being fools? How long will you scoff at wisdom and fight the facts? [23] Come here and listen to me! I'll pour out the spirit of Wisdom upon you, and make you wise. [24] I have called you so often but still you won't come. I have pleaded, but all in vain. [25] For you have spurned my counsel and reproof. [26] Some day you'll be in trouble, and I'll laugh! Mock me, will you? — I'll mock you! [27] When a storm of terror surrounds you, and when you are engulfed by anguish and distress, [28] Then I will not answer your cry for help. It will be too late though you search for me ever so anxiously.

[29] "For you closed your eyes to the facts and did not choose to reverence and trust the Lord, [30] And you turned your back on me, spurning my advice. [31] That is why you must eat the bitter fruit of having your own way, and experience the full terrors of the pathway you have chosen. [32] For you turned away from me — to death; your own complacency will kill you. Fools! [33] But all who listen to me shall live in peace and safety, unafraid."

Psalms for the Second Day

6 No, Lord! Don't punish me in the heat of Your anger. ² Pity me, O Lord, for I am weak. Heal me, for my body is sick, ³ And I am upset and disturbed. My mind is filled with apprehension and with gloom. Oh, restore me soon.

⁴ Come, O Lord, and make me well. In Your kindness save me. ⁵ For if I die I cannot give You glory by praising You before my friends. ⁶ I am worn out with pain; every night my pillow is wet with tears. ⁷ My eyes are growing old and dim with grief because of all my enemies.

⁸ Go, leave me now, you men of evil deeds, for the Lord has heard my weeping ⁹ And my pleading. He will answer all my prayers. ¹⁰ All my enemies shall be suddenly dishonored, terror-stricken, and disgraced. God will turn them back in shame.

7 I am depending on You, O Lord my God, to save me from my persecutors. ² Don't let them pounce upon me as a lion would and maul me and drag me away with no one to rescue me. ³ It would be different, Lord, if I were doing evil things — ⁴ If I were paying back evil for good or unjustly attacking those I dislike. ⁵ Then it would be right for You to let my enemies destroy me, crush me to the ground, and trample my life in the dust.

6 But Lord! Arise in anger against the anger of my enemies. Awake! Demand justice for me, Lord! 7, 8 Gather all peoples before You; sit high above them, judging their sins. But justify me publicly; establish my honor and truth before them all. 9 End all wickedness, O Lord, and bless all who truly worship God; for You, the righteous God, look deep within the hearts of men and examine all their motives and their thoughts.

10 God is my shield; He will defend me. He saves those whose hearts and lives are true and right.

11 God is a judge who is perfectly fair, and He is angry with the wicked every day. 12 Unless they repent, He will sharpen His sword and slay them. He has bent and strung His bow 13 And fitted it with deadly arrows made from shafts of fire.

14 The wicked man conceives an evil plot, labors with its dark details, and brings to birth his treachery and lies; 15 Let him fall into his own trap. 16 May the violence he plans for others boomerang upon himself; let him die.

17 Oh, how grateful and thankful I am to the Lord because He is so good. I will sing praise to the name of the Lord who is above all lords.

8 O Lord our God, the majesty and glory of Your name fills all the earth and overflows the heavens. 2 You have taught the little children to praise You perfectly. May their example shame and silence Your enemies!

³ When I look up into the night skies and see the work of Your fingers — the moon and the stars You have made — ⁴ I cannot understand how You can bother with mere puny man, to pay any attention to him! ⁵ And yet You have made him only a little lower than the angels, and placed a crown of glory and honor upon his head. ⁶ You have put him in charge of everything You made; everything is put under his authority: ⁷ All sheep and oxen, and wild animals too, ⁸ The birds and fish, and all the life in the sea. ⁹ O Jehovah, our Lord, the majesty and glory of Your name fills the earth.

9 O Lord, I will praise You with all my heart, and tell everyone about the marvelous things You do. ² I will be glad, yes, filled with joy because of You. I will sing Your praises, O Lord God above all gods.

³ My enemies will fall back and perish in Your presence; ⁴ You have vindicated me; You have endorsed my work, declaring from Your throne that it is good. ⁵ You have rebuked the nations and destroyed the wicked, blotting out their names for ever and ever. ⁶ O enemies of mine, you are doomed forever. The Lord will destroy your cities; even the memory of them will disappear.

⁷, ⁸ But the Lord lives on forever; He sits upon His throne to judge justly the nations of the world. ⁹ All who are oppressed may come to Him. He is a refuge for them in their times of trouble. ¹⁰ All those who know Your mercy, Lord, will count on You for help. For You have never yet forsaken those who trust in You.

¹¹ Oh, sing out your praises to the God who lives in Jerusalem. Tell the world about His unforgettable

deeds. [12] He who avenges murder has an open ear to those who cry to Him for justice. He does not ignore the prayers of men in trouble when they call to Him for help.

[13] And now, O Lord, have mercy on me; see how I suffer at the hands of those who hate me. Lord, snatch me back from the jaws of death. [14] Save me, so that I can praise You publicly before all the people at Jerusalem's gates and rejoice that You have rescued me.

[15] The nations fall into the pitfalls they have dug for others; the trap they set has snapped on them. [16] The Lord is famous for the way He punishes the wicked in their own snares!

[17] The wicked shall be sent away to hell; this is the fate of all the nations forgetting the Lord. [18] For the needs of the needy shall not be ignored forever; the hopes of the poor shall not always be crushed.

[19] O Lord, arise and judge and punish the nations; don't let them conquer You! [20] Make them tremble in fear; put the nations in their place until at last they know they are but puny men.

10 Lord, why are You standing aloof and far away? Why do you hide when I need You the most?

[2] Come and deal with all these proud and wicked men who viciously persecute the poor. Pour upon these men the evil they planned for others! [3] For these men brag of all their evil lusts; they revile God and congratulate those the Lord abhors, whose only goal in life is money.

⁴ These wicked men, so proud and haughty, seem to think that God is dead. They wouldn't think of looking for Him! ⁵ Yet there is success in everything they do, and their enemies fall before them. They do not see Your punishment awaiting them. ⁶ They boast that neither God nor man can ever keep them down — somehow they'll find a way!

⁷ Their mouths are full of profanity and lies and fraud. They are always boasting of their evil plans. ⁸ They lurk in dark alleys of the city and murder passersby. ⁹ Like lions they crouch silently, waiting to pounce upon the poor. Like hunters they catch their victims in their traps. ¹⁰ The unfortunate are overwhelmed by their superior strength and fall beneath their blows. ¹¹ "God isn't watching," they say to themselves; "He'll never know!"

¹² O Lord, arise! O God, crush them! Don't forget the poor or anyone else in need. ¹³ Why do You let the wicked get away with this contempt for God? For they think that God will never call them to account. ¹⁴ Lord, You see what they are doing. You have noted each evil act. You know what trouble and grief they have caused. Now punish them. O Lord, the poor man trusts himself to You; You are known as the helper of the helpless. ¹⁵ Break the arms of these wicked men. Go after them until the last of them is destroyed.

¹⁶ The Lord is King forever and forever. Those who follow other gods shall be swept from His land.

¹⁷ Lord, You know the hopes of humble people. Surely You will hear their cries and comfort their hearts by helping them. ¹⁸ You will be with the orphans and all who are oppressed, so that mere earthly man will terrify them no longer.

Proverbs for the Second Day

2 Every young man who listens to me and obeys my instructions will be given wisdom and good sense. [3, 4, 5] Yes, if you want better insight and discernment, and are searching for them as you would for lost money or hidden treasure, then wisdom will be given you and knowledge of God Himself; you will soon learn the importance of reverence for the Lord and of trusting Him.

[6] For the Lord grants wisdom! His every word is a treasure of knowledge and understanding. [7, 8] He grants good sense to the godly — His saints. He is their shield, protecting them and guarding their pathway. [9] He shows how to distinguish right from wrong, how to find the right decision every time. [10] For wisdom and truth will enter the very center of your being, filling your life with joy. [11, 12, 13] You will be given the sense to stay away from evil men who want you to be their partners in crime — men who turn from God's ways to walk down dark and evil paths, [14] And exult in doing wrong, for they thoroughly enjoy their sins. [15] Everything they do is crooked and wrong.

[16, 17] Only wisdom from the Lord can save a man from the flattery of prostitutes; these girls have abandoned their husbands and flouted the laws of God.

¹⁸ Their houses lie along the road to death and hell. ¹⁹ The men who enter them are doomed. None of these men will ever be the same again.

²⁰ Follow the steps of the godly instead, and stay on the right path, ²¹ For only good men enjoy life to the full; ²² Evil men lose the good things they might have had; and they themselves shall be destroyed.

Psalms for the Third Day

11 How dare you tell me, "Flee to the mountains for safety," when I am trusting in the Lord?

² For the wicked have strung their bows, drawn their arrows tight against the bowstrings, and aimed from ambush at the people of God. ³ "Law and order have collapsed," we are told. "What can the righteous do but flee?"

⁴ But the Lord is still in His holy temple; He still rules from heaven. He closely watches everything that happens here on earth. ⁵ He puts the righteous and the wicked to the test; He hates those loving violence. ⁶ He will rain down fire and brimstone on the wicked and scorch them with His burning wind.

⁷ For God is good, and He loves goodness; the godly shall see His face.

12 Lord! Help! Godly men are fast disappearing. Where in all the world can dependable men be found? ² Everyone deceives and flatters and lies. There is no sincerity left.

³, ⁴ But the Lord will not deal gently with people who act like that; He will destroy those proud liars who say, "We will lie to our hearts' content. Our lips are our own; who can stop us?"

⁵ The Lord replies, "I will arise and defend the oppressed, the poor, the needy. I will rescue them as they have longed for Me to do." ⁶ The Lord's promise is sure. He speaks no careless word; all He says is purest truth, like silver seven times refined. ⁷ O Lord, we know that You will forever preserve Your own from the reach of evil men, ⁸ Although they prowl on every side and vileness is praised throughout the land.

13 How long will You forget me, Lord? Forever? How long will You look the other way when I am in need? ² How long must I be hiding daily anguish in my heart? How long shall my enemy have the upper hand? ³ Answer me, O Lord my God; give me light in my darkness lest I die. ⁴ Don't let my enemies say, "We have conquered him!" Don't let them gloat that I am down.

⁵ But I will always trust in You and in Your mercy and shall rejoice in Your salvation. ⁶ I will sing to the Lord because He has blessed me so richly.

14 That man is a fool who says to himself, "There is no God!" Anyone who talks like that is warped and evil and cannot really be a good person at all.

² The Lord looks down from heaven on all mankind to see if there are any who are wise, who want to please God. ³ But no, all have strayed away; all are rotten with sin. Not one is good, not one! ⁴ They eat my people like bread and wouldn't think of praying! Don't they really know any better?

⁵ Terror shall grip them, for God is with those who love Him. ⁶ He is the refuge of the poor and humble when evildoers are oppressing them. ⁷ Oh, that the time of their rescue were already here; that God would

come from Zion now to save His people. What gladness when the Lord has rescued Israel!

15 Lord, who may go and find refuge and shelter in Your tabernacle up on Your holy hill?

² Anyone who leads a blameless life and is truly sincere. ³ Anyone who refuses to slander others, does not listen to gossip, never harms his neighbor, ⁴ Speaks out against sin, criticizes those committing it, commends the faithful followers of the Lord, keeps a promise even if it ruins him, ⁵ Does not crush his debtors with high interest rates, and refuses to testify against the innocent despite the bribes offered him — such a man shall stand firm forever.

Proverbs for the Third Day

3 My son, never forget the things I've taught you. If you want a long and satisfying life, closely follow my instructions. ³ Never forget to be truthful and kind. Hold these virtues tightly. Write them deep within your heart. ⁴, ⁵ If you want favor with both God and man, and a reputation for good judgment and common sense, then trust the Lord completely; don't ever trust yourself. ⁶ In everything you do, put God first, and He will direct you and crown your efforts with success.

⁷, ⁸ Don't be conceited, sure of your own wisdom. Instead, trust and reverence the Lord, and turn your back on evil; when you do that, then you will be given renewed health and vitality.

⁹, ¹⁰ Honor the Lord by giving Him the first part of all your income, and He will fill your barns with wheat and barley and overflow your wine vats with the finest wines.

¹¹, ¹² Young man, do not resent it when God chastens and corrects you, for His punishment is proof of His love. Just as a father punishes a son he delights in to make him better, so the Lord corrects you.

¹³, ¹⁴, ¹⁵ The man who knows right from wrong and has good judgment and common sense is happier than

the man who is immensely rich! For such wisdom is
far more valuable than precious jewels. Nothing else
compares with it. ¹⁶, ¹⁷ Wisdom gives:

A long, good life

Riches   Pleasure

Honor   Peace

¹⁸ Wisdom is a tree of life to those who eat her fruit;
happy is the man who keeps on eating it.

¹⁹ The Lord's wisdom founded the earth; His understanding established all the universe and space.

²⁰ The deep fountains of the earth were broken open
by His knowledge, and the skies poured down rain.

²¹ Have two goals: wisdom — that is, knowing and
doing right — and common sense. Don't let them slip
away, ²² For they fill you with living energy, and are
a feather in your cap. ²³ They keep you safe from
defeat and disaster and from stumbling off the trail.
²⁴, ²⁵, ²⁶ With them on guard you can sleep without
fear; and you need not be afraid of disaster or the
plots of wicked men; for the Lord is with you; He protects you.

²⁷, ²⁸ Don't withhold repayment of your debts.
Don't say, "Some other time," if you can pay now.
²⁹ Don't plot against your neighbor; he is trusting
you. ³⁰ Don't get into needless fights. ³¹ Don't envy
violent men. Don't copy their ways. ³² For such men
are an abomination to the Lord, but He gives His
friendship to the godly.

³³ The curse of God is on the wicked, but His blessing is on the upright. ³⁴ The Lord mocks at mockers,
but helps the humble. ³⁵ The wise are promoted to
honor, but fools are promoted to shame!

Psalms for the Fourth Day

16   Save me, O God, because I have come to You for refuge. ² I said to Him, "You are my Lord; I have no other help but Yours." ³ I want the company of the godly men and women in the land; they are the true nobility. ⁴ Those choosing other gods shall all be filled with sorrow; I will not offer the sacrifices they do or even speak the names of their gods.

⁵ The Lord Himself is my inheritance, my prize! He is my food and drink, my highest joy! He guards all that is mine. ⁶ He sees that I am given pleasant brooks and meadows as my share! What a wonderful inheritance! ⁷ I will bless the Lord who counsels me; He gives me wisdom in the night. He tells me what to do.

⁸ I am always thinking of the Lord; and because He is so near, I never need to stumble or to fall. ⁹ Heart, body, and soul are filled with joy. ¹⁰ For You will not leave me among the dead; You will not allow Your beloved one to rot in the grave. ¹¹ You have let me experience the joys of life and the exquisite pleasures of Your own eternal presence.

17   I am pleading for Your help, O Lord; for I have been honest and have done what is right, and You must listen to my earnest cry! ² Publicly acquit me,

Lord, for You are always fair. ³ You have tested me
and seen that I am good. You have come even in the
night and found nothing amiss and know that I have
told the truth. ⁴ I have followed Your commands and
have not gone along with cruel and evil men. ⁵ My
feet have not slipped from Your paths.

⁶ Why am I praying like this? Because I know You
will answer me, O God! Yes, listen as I pray. ⁷ Show
me Your strong love in wonderful ways, O Savior of
all those seeking Your help against their foes. ⁸ Protect me as You would the pupil of Your eye; hide me
in the shadow of Your wings as You hover over me.

⁹ My enemies encircle me with murder in their
eyes. ¹⁰ They are pitiless and arrogant. Listen to
their boasting. ¹¹ They close in upon me and are
ready to throw me to the ground. ¹² They are like
lions eager to tear me apart, like young lions hiding
and waiting their chance.

¹³, ¹⁴ Lord, arise and stand against them! Push
them back! Come and save me from these men of the
world whose only concern is earthly gain — these men
whom You have filled with Your treasures so that
their children and grandchildren are rich and prosperous.

¹⁵ But as for me, my contentment is not in wealth
but in seeing You and knowing all is well between us.
And when I awake in heaven, I will be fully satisfied,
for I will see You face to face.

*(This song of David was written at a time when the
Lord had delivered him from his many enemies, in-
cluding Saul.)*

18   Lord, how I love You! For You have done such
tremendous things for me.

² The Lord is my fort where I can enter and be
safe; no one can follow me in and slay me. He is a
rugged mountain where I hide; He is my Savior, a
rock where none can reach me, and a tower of safety.
He is my shield. He is like the strong horn of a mighty
fighting bull. ³ All I need to do is cry to Him — oh,
praise the Lord — and I am saved from all my enemies!

⁴ Death bound me with chains, and the floods of
ungodliness mounted a massive attack against me.
⁵ Trapped and helpless, I struggled against the ropes
that drew me on to death.

⁶ In my distress I screamed to the Lord for His
help. And He heard me from heaven; my cry reached
His ears. ⁷ Then the earth rocked and reeled, and
mountains shook and trembled. How they quaked!
For He was angry. ⁸ Fierce flames leaped from His
mouth, setting fire to the earth; smoke blew from His
nostrils. ⁹ He bent the heavens down and came to
my defense; thick darkness was beneath His feet.
¹⁰ Mounted on the cherubim He sped swiftly to my
aid with wings of wind. ¹¹ He enshrouded Himself
with darkness, veiling His approach with dense
clouds dark as murky waters. ¹² Suddenly the bril-
liance of His presence broke through the clouds with
lightning and a mighty storm of hail.

¹³ The Lord thundered in the heavens; the God
above all gods has spoken — oh, the hailstones; oh,
the fire! ¹⁴ He flashed His fearful arrows of lightning
and routed all my enemies. See how they run! ¹⁵ Then
at Your command, O Lord, the sea receded from the

shore. At the blast of Your breath the depths were laid bare.

16 He reached down from heaven and took me and drew me out of my great trials. He rescued me from deep waters. 17 He delivered me from my strong enemy, from those who hated me — I who was helpless in their hands.

18 On the day when I was weakest, they attacked. But the Lord held me steady. 19 He led me to a place of safety, for He delights in me. 20 The Lord rewarded me for doing right and being pure. 21 For I have followed His commands and have not sinned by turning back from following Him. 22 I kept close watch on all His laws; I did not refuse a single one. 23 I did my best to keep them all, holding myself back from doing wrong. 24 And so the Lord has paid me with His blessings, for I have done what is right, and I am pure of heart. This He knows, for He watches my every step.

25 Lord, how merciful You are to those who are merciful. And You do not punish those who run from evil. 26 You give blessings to the pure but pain to those who leave Your paths. 27 You deliver the humble but condemn the proud and haughty ones. 28 You have turned on my light! The Lord my God has made my darkness turn to light. 29 Now in Your strength I can scale any wall, attack any troop.

30 What a God He is! How perfect in every way! All His promises prove true. He is a shield for everyone who hides behind Him. 31 For who is God except our Lord? Who but He is as a rock?

³² He fills me with strength and protects me wherever I go. ³³ He gives me the surefootedness of a mountain goat upon the crags. He leads me safely along the top of the cliffs. ³⁴ He prepares me for battle and gives me strength to drawn an iron bow!

³⁵ You have given me Your salvation as my shield. Your right hand, O Lord, supports me; Your gentleness has made me great. ³⁶ You have made wide steps beneath my feet so that I need never slip. ³⁷ I chased my enemies; I caught up with them and did not turn back until all were conquered. ³⁸ I pinned them to the ground; all were helpless before me. I placed my feet upon their necks! ³⁹ For You have armed me with strong armor for the battle. My enemies quail before me and fall defeated at my feet. ⁴⁰ You made them turn and run; I destroyed all who hated me. ⁴¹ They shouted for help but no one dared to rescue them; they cried to the Lord, but He refused to answer them. ⁴² So I crushed them fine as dust and cast them to the wind. I threw them away like sweepings from the floor. ^{43, 44, 45} You gave me victory in every battle! The nations came and served me. Even those I didn't know before come now and bow before me. Foreigners who have never seen me submit instantly. They come trembling from their strongholds.

⁴⁶ God is alive! Praise Him who is the great rock of protection. ⁴⁷ He is the God who pays back those who harm me and subdues the nations before me.

⁴⁸ He rescues me from my enemies; He holds me safely out of their reach and saves me from these powerful opponents. ⁴⁹ For this, O Lord, I will praise You among the nations. ⁵⁰ Many times You have miraculously rescued me, the king You appointed.

You have been loving and kind to me and will be to my descendants.

19 The heavens are telling the glory of God; they are a marvelous display of His craftsmanship. [2] Day and night they keep on telling about God. [3, 4] Without a sound or word, silent in the skies, their message reaches out to all the world. The sun lives in the heavens where God placed it [5] And moves out across the skies as radiant as a bridegroom going to his wedding, or as joyous as an athlete looking forward to a race! [6] The sun crosses the heavens from end to end, and nothing can hide from its heat.

[7, 8] God's laws are perfect. They protect us, make us wise, and give us joy and light. [9] God's laws are just and perfect. Reverence for God keeps us pure and leads us on to heaven. [10] His laws are more desirable than gold. They are sweeter than honey dripping from a honeycomb. [11] For they warn us away from harm and give success to those who obey them!

[12] But how can I ever know what sins are lurking in my heart? Cleanse me from these hidden faults. [13] And keep me from deliberate wrongs; help me to stop doing them. Only then can I be free of guilt and innocent of some great crime.

[14] May my spoken words and unspoken thoughts be pleasing even to You, O Lord my Rock and my Redeemer.

20 In your day of trouble, may the Lord be with you! May the God of Jacob keep you from all harm. [2] May He send you aid from His sanctuary in Zion. [3] May He remember with pleasure the gifts you have given Him, your sacrifices and burnt offerings. [4] May

He grant you your heart's desire and fulfill all your plans. ⁵ May there be shouts of joy when we hear the news of your victory, flags flying with praise to God for all that He has done for you. May He answer all your prayers!

⁶ "God save the king" — I know He does! He hears me from highest heaven and sends great victories. ⁷ Some nations boast of armies and of weaponry, but our boast is in the Lord our God. ⁸ Those nations will collapse and perish; we will arise to stand firm and sure!

⁹ Give victory to our king, O Lord; oh, hear our prayer.

Proverbs for the Fourth Day

4 Young men, listen to me as you would to your father. Listen, and grow wise, for I speak the truth — don't turn away. ³ For I, too, was once a son, tenderly loved by my mother as an only child, and the companion of my father. ⁴ He told me never to forget his words, "If you follow them," he said, "you will have a long and happy life." ⁵ *"Learn to be wise,"* he said, *and develop good judgment and common sense! I cannot overemphasize this point."* ⁶ Cling to wisdom — she will protect you. Love her — she will guard you.

⁷ Determination to be wise is the first step toward becoming wise! And with your wisdom, develop common sense and good judgment. ⁸, ⁹ If you exalt wisdom, she will exalt you. Hold her fast and she will lead you to great honor; she will place a beautiful crown upon your head. ¹⁰ My son, listen to me and do as I say, and you will have a long, good life.

¹¹ I would have you learn this great fact: that a life of doing right is the wisest life there is. ¹² If you live that kind of life, you'll not limp or stumble as you run. ¹³ Carry out my instructions; don't forget them, for they will lead you to real living.

¹⁴ Don't do as the wicked do. ¹⁵ Avoid their haunts — turn away, go somewhere else, ¹⁶ For evil men don't

sleep until they've done their evil deed for the day. They can't rest unless they cause someone to stumble and fall. ¹⁷ They eat and drink wickedness and violence!

¹⁸ But the good man walks along in the ever brightening light of God's favor; the dawn gives way to morning splendor, ¹⁹ While the evil man gropes and stumbles in the dark.

²⁰ Listen, son of mine, to what I say. Listen carefully. ²¹ Keep these thoughts ever in mind; let them penetrate deep within your heart: ²² For they will mean real life for you, and radiant health.

²³ *Above all else, guard your affections.* For they influence everything else in your life. ²⁴ Spurn the careless kiss of a prostitute. Stay far from her. ²⁵ Look straight ahead; don't even turn your head to look. ²⁶ Watch your step. Stick to the path and be safe. ²⁷ Don't side-track; pull back your foot from danger.

Psalms for the Fifth Day

21 How the king rejoices in Your strength, O Lord! How he exults in Your salvation. ² For You have given him his heart's desire, everything he asks You for!

³ You welcomed him to the throne with success and prosperity. You set a kingly crown of purest gold upon his head. ⁴ He asked for a long, good life, and You have granted his request; the days of his life stretch on and on forever! ⁵ You have given him fame and honor. You have clothed him with splendor and majesty. ⁶ You have endowed him with eternal happiness. You have given him the unquenchable joy of Your presence. ⁷ And because the king trusts in the Lord, he will never stumble, never fall; for he depends upon the steadfast love of the God who is above all gods.

⁸ Your hand, O Lord, will find Your enemies, all who hate You. ⁹, ¹⁰ When You appear, they will be destroyed in the fierce fire of Your presence. The Lord will destroy them and their children. ¹¹ For these men plot against You, Lord, but they cannot possibly succeed. ¹² They will turn and flee when they see Your arrows aimed straight at them.

¹³ Accept our praise, O Lord, for all Your glorious

power! We will write songs to celebrate Your mighty acts!

22   My God, my God, why have You forsaken me? Why do You refuse to help me or even to listen to my groans? ² Day and night I keep on weeping, crying for Your help, but there is no reply — ³, ⁴ For *You are holy.*

The praises of our fathers surrounded Your throne; they trusted You and You delivered them. ⁵ You heard their cries for help and saved them; they were never disappointed when they sought Your aid.

⁶ But I am a worm, not a man, scorned and despised by my own people and by all mankind. ⁷ Everyone who sees me mocks and sneers and shrugs. ⁸ "Is this the one who rolled his burden on the Lord?" they laugh. "Is this the one who claims the Lord delights in him? We'll believe it when we see God rescue him!"

⁹, ¹⁰, ¹¹ Lord, how You have helped me before! You took me safely from my mother's womb and brought me through the years of infancy. I have depended upon You since birth; You have always been my God. Don't leave me now, for trouble is near and no one else can possibly help.

¹² I am surrounded by fearful enemies, strong as the giant bulls from Bashan. ¹³ They come at me with open jaws, like roaring lions attacking their prey. ¹⁴ My strength has drained away like water, and all my bones are out of joint. My heart melts like wax; ¹⁵ My strength has dried up like sun-baked clay; my tongue sticks to my mouth, for You have laid me in the dust of death. ¹⁶ The enemy, this gang of evil men, circles me like a pack of dogs; they have pierced

my hands and feet. ¹⁷ I can count every bone in my body. See these men of evil gloat and stare; ¹⁸ They divide my clothes among themselves by a toss of the dice.

¹⁹ O Lord, don't stay away. O God my Strength, hurry to my aid. ²⁰ Rescue me from death; spare my precious life from all these evil men. ²¹ Save me from these lions' jaws and from the horns of these wild oxen; yes, God will answer me and rescue me.

²² I will praise You to all my brothers; I will stand up before the congregation and testify of the wonderful things You have done. ²³ "Praise the Lord, each one of you who fears Him," I will say. "Each of you must fear and reverence His name. Let all Israel sing His praises, ²⁴ For He has not despised my cries of deep despair; He has not turned and walked away. When I cried to Him, He heard and came."

²⁵ Yes, I will stand and praise You before all the people. I will publicly fulfill my vows in the presence of all who reverence Your name.

²⁶ The poor shall eat and be satisfied; all who seek the Lord shall find Him and shall praise His name. Their hearts shall rejoice with everlasting joy. ²⁷ The whole earth shall see it and return to the Lord; the people of every nation shall worship Him.

²⁸ For the Lord is King and rules the nations. ²⁹ Both proud and humble together, all who are mortal — born to die — shall worship Him. ³⁰ Our children too shall serve Him, for they shall hear from us about the wonders of the Lord; ³¹ Generations yet unborn shall hear of all the miracles He did for us.

23   Because the Lord is my shepherd, I have everything I need!

2, 3   He lets me rest in the meadow grass and leads me beside the quiet streams. He restores my failing health. He helps me do what honors Him the most.

4 Even when walking through the Dark Valley of death I will not be afraid, for You are close beside me, guarding, guiding all the way.

5 You provide delicious food for me in the presence of my enemies. You have welcomed me as Your guest; blessings overflow!

6 Your goodness and unfailing kindness shall be with me all of my life, and afterwards I will live with You forever in Your home.

24   The earth belongs to God! Everything in all the world is His! 2 He is the One who pushed the oceans back to let dry land appear.

3 Who may climb the mountain of the Lord and enter where He lives? Who may stand before the Lord? 4 Only those with pure hands and hearts, who do not practice dishonesty and lying. 5 They will receive God's own goodness as their blessing from Him, planted in their lives by God Himself, their Savior. 6 These are the ones who are allowed to stand before the Lord and worship the God of Jacob.

7 Open up, O ancient gates, and let the King of Glory in. 8 Who is this King of Glory? The Lord, strong and mighty, invincible in battle. 9 Yes, open wide the gates and let the King of Glory in.

10 Who is this King of Glory? The Commander of all of heaven's armies!

25 To You, O Lord, I pray! ² Don't fail me, Lord, for I am trusting You. Don't let my enemies succeed. Don't give them victory over me.

³ None who have faith in God will ever be disgraced for trusting Him. But all who harm the innocent shall be defeated.

⁴ Show me the path where I should go, O Lord; point out the right road for me to walk. ⁵ Lead me; teach me; for You are the God who gives me salvation. I have no hope except in You. ⁶, ⁷ Overlook my youthful sins, O Lord! Look at me instead through eyes of mercy and forgiveness, through eyes of everlasting love and kindness.

⁸ The Lord is good and glad to teach the proper path to all who go astray; ⁹ He will teach the ways that are right and best to those who humbly turn to Him. ¹⁰ And when we obey Him, every path He guides us on is fragrant with His lovingkindness and His truth.

¹¹ But Lord, my sins! How many they are. Oh, pardon them for the honor of Your name.

¹²Where is the man who fears the Lord? God will teach him how to choose the best!

¹³ He shall live within God's circle of blessing, and his children shall inherit the earth!

¹⁴ Friendship with God is reserved for those who reverence Him. With them alone He shares the secrets of His promises.

¹⁵ My eyes are ever looking to the Lord for help, for He alone can rescue me. ¹⁶ Come, Lord, and show me Your mercy, for I am helpless, overwhelmed, in deep

distress; ¹⁷ My problems go from bad to worse. Oh, save me from them all! ¹⁸ See my sorrows; feel my pain; forgive my sins. ¹⁹ See how many enemies I have and how viciously they hate me! ²⁰ Save me from them! Deliver my life from their power! Oh, let it never be said that I trusted You in vain!

²¹ Assign me Godliness and Integrity as my body-guards, for I expect You to protect me, ²² And to ransom Israel from all her troubles.

Proverbs for the Fifth Day

5 Listen to me, my son! I know what I am saying; *listen!* [2] Watch yourself, lest you be indiscreet and betray some vital information. [3] For the lips of a prostitute are as sweet as honey, and smooth flattery is her stock in trade. [4] But afterwards only a bitter conscience is left to you, sharp as a double-edged sword. [5] She leads you down to death and hell. [6] For she does not know the path to life. She staggers down a crooked trail, and doesn't even realize where it leads.

[7] Young man, listen to me, and never forget what I'm about to say: [8] *Run from her! Don't go near her house,* [9] Lest you fall to her temptation and lose your honor, and give the remainder of your life to the cruel and merciless; [10] Lest strangers obtain your wealth, and you become a slave of foreigners. [11] Lest afterwards you groan in anguish and in shame, when syphilis consumes your body, [12] And you say, "Oh, if only I had listened! If only I had not demanded my own way! [13] Oh, why wouldn't I take advice? Why was I so stupid? [14] For now I must face public disgrace."

[15] Drink from your own well, my son — be faithful and true to your wife. [16] Why should you beget children with women of the street? [17] Why share your children with those outside your home? [18] Let your

manhood be a blessing, rejoice in the wife of your youth. ¹⁹ Let her charms and tender embrace satisfy you. Let her love alone fill you with delight. ²⁰ Why delight yourself with prostitutes, embracing what isn't yours? ²¹ *For God is closely watching you,* and He weighs carefully everything you do.

²² The wicked man is doomed by his own sins; they are ropes that catch and hold him. ²³ He shall die because he will not listen to the truth; he has let himself be led away into incredible folly.

Psalms for the Sixth Day

26 Dismiss all the charges against me, Lord, for I have tried to keep Your laws and have trusted You without wavering. ² Cross-examine me, O Lord, and see that this is so; test my motives and affections too. ³ For I have taken Your lovingkindness and Your truth as my ideals. ⁴ I do not have fellowship with tricky, two-faced men; they are false and hypocritical. ⁵ I hate the sinners' hangouts and refuse to enter them. ⁶ I wash my hands to prove my innocence and come before Your altar ⁷ Singing a song of thanksgiving and telling about Your miracles.

⁸ Lord, I love Your home, this shrine where the brilliant, dazzling splendor of Your presence lives.

⁹, ¹⁰ Don't treat me as a common sinner or murderer who plots against the innocent and demands bribes. ¹¹ No, I am not like that, O Lord; I try to walk a straight and narrow path of doing what is right; therefore in mercy save me.

¹² I publicly praise the Lord for keeping me from slipping and falling.

27 The Lord is my light and my salvation; whom shall I fear? ² When evil men come to destroy me, they will stumble and fall! ³ Yes, though a mighty army marches against me, my heart shall know no fear! I am confident that God will save me.

⁴ The one thing I want from God, the thing I seek most of all, is the privilege of meditating in His temple, living in His presence every day of my life, delighting in His incomparable perfections and glory. ⁵ There I'll be when troubles come! He will hide me. He will set me on a high rock ⁶ Out of reach of all my enemies. Then I will bring Him sacrifices and sing His praises with much joy. ⁷ Listen to my pleading, Lord! Be merciful and send the help I need.

⁸ My heart has heard You say, "Come and talk with Me, O My people." And my heart responds, "Lord, I am coming."

⁹ Oh, do not hide Yourself when I am trying to find You. Do not angrily reject Your servant! You have been my help in all my trials before; don't leave me now. Don't forsake me, O God of my salvation. ¹⁰ For if my father and mother should abandon me, You would welcome and comfort me.

¹¹ Tell me what to do, O Lord, and make it plain because I am surrounded by waiting enemies. ¹² Don't let them get me, Lord! Don't let me fall into their hands! For they accuse me of things I never did, and all the while are plotting cruelty. ¹³ I am expecting the Lord to rescue me again, so that once again I will see His goodness to me here in the land of the living!

¹⁴ Don't be impatient! Wait for the Lord, and He will come and save you! Be brave, stout-hearted and courageous. Yes, wait and He will help you.

28   I plead with You to help me, Lord, for You are my Rock of safety. If you refuse to answer me, I might as well give up and die. ² Lord, I lift my hands to heaven and implore Your help. Oh, listen to my cry.

³ Don't punish me with all the wicked ones who speak so sweetly to their neighbors while planning to murder them. ⁴ Give them the punishment they so richly deserve! Measure it out to them in proportion to their wickedness; pay them back for all their evil deeds. ⁵ They care nothing for God or what He has done or what He has made; therefore God will dismantle them like old buildings, never to be rebuilt again.

⁶ Oh, praise the Lord, for He has listened to my pleadings! ⁷ He is my strength, my shield from every danger. I trusted in Him, and He helped me! Joy rises in my heart until I burst out in songs of praise to Him. ⁸ The Lord protects His people and gives victory to His anointed king.

⁹ Defend Your people, Lord; defend and bless Your chosen ones. Lead them like a shepherd and carry them forever in Your arms.

29   Praise the Lord, you angels of His; praise His glory and His strength. ² Praise Him for His majestic glory, the glory of His name. Come before Him clothed in sacred garments.

³ The voice of the Lord echoes from the clouds. The God of Glory thunders through the skies. ⁴ So powerful is His voice; so full of majesty. ⁵, ⁶ It breaks down the cedars! It splits the giant trees of Lebanon. It shakes Mount Lebanon and Mount Sirion. They leap and skip before Him like young calves! ⁷ The voice

of the Lord thunders through the lightning. ⁸ It resounds through the deserts and shakes the wilderness of Kadesh. ⁹ The voice of the Lord spins and topples the mighty oaks. It strips the forests bare! They whirl and sway beneath the blast. But in His temple all are praising, "Glory, glory to the Lord."

¹⁰ At the Flood, the Lord showed His control of all creation. Now He continues to unveil His power. ¹¹ He will give His people strength. He will bless them with peace.

30 I will praise You, Lord, for You have saved me from my enemies. You refuse to let them triumph over me. ² O Lord my God, I pled with You, and You gave me my health again. ³ You brought me back from the brink of the grave, from death itself, and here I am alive!

⁴ Oh, sing to Him you saints of His; give thanks to His holy name. ⁵ His anger lasts a moment; His favor lasts for life! Weeping may go on all night, but in the morning there is joy.

⁶, ⁷ In my prosperity I said, "This is forever; nothing can stop me now! The Lord has shown me His favor. He has made me steady as a mountain." Then, Lord, You turned Your face away from me and cut off Your river of blessings. Suddenly my courage was gone; I was terrified and panic-stricken. ⁸ I cried to You, O Lord; oh, how I pled: ⁹ "What will You gain, O Lord, from killing me? How can I praise You then to all my friends? How can my dust in the grave speak out and tell the world about Your faithfulness? ¹⁰ Hear me, Lord; oh, have pity and help me." ¹¹ Then He turned my sorrow into joy! He took away

my clothes of mourning and gave me gay and festive garments to rejoice in [12] So that I might sing glad praises to the Lord instead of lying in silence in the grave. O Lord my God, I will keep on thanking You forever!

Proverbs for the Sixth Day

6 Son, if you endorse a note for someone you hardly know, guaranteeing his debt, you are in serious trouble. [2] You may have trapped yourself by your agreement. [3] Quick! Get out of it if you possibly can! Swallow your pride; don't let embarrassment stand in the way. Go and beg to have your name erased. [4] Don't put it off. Do it now. Don't rest until you do. [5] If you can get out of this trap you have saved yourself like a deer that escapes from a hunter, or a bird from the net.

[6] Take a lesson from the ants, you lazy fellow. Learn from their ways and be wise! [7] For though they have no king to make them work, [8] Yet they labor hard all summer, gathering food for the winter. [9] But you — all you do is sleep. When will you wake up? [10] "Let me sleep a little longer!" Sure, just a little more! [11] And as you sleep, poverty creeps upon you like a robber and destroys you; want attacks you in full armor.

[12, 13] Let me describe for you a worthless and a wicked man; first, he is a constant liar; he signals his true intentions to his friends with eyes and feet and fingers. [14] Next, his heart is full of rebellion. And he spends his time thinking of all the evil he can do, and

stirring up discontent. ¹⁵ But he will be destroyed suddenly, broken beyond hope of healing.

¹⁶⁻¹⁹ For there are six things the Lord hates — no, seven:

> Haughtiness
> Lying
> Murdering
> Plotting evil
> Eagerness to do wrong
> A false witness
> Sowing discord among brothers

²⁰ Young man, obey your father and your mother. ²¹ Tie their instructions around your finger so you won't forget. Take to heart all of their advice. ²² Every day and all night long their counsel will lead you and save you from harm; when you wake up in the morning, let their instructions guide you into the new day. ²³ For their advice is a beam of light directed into the dark corners of your mind to warn you of danger and to give you a good life. ²⁴ Their counsel will keep you far away from prostitutes with all their flatteries.

²⁵ Don't lust for her beauty. Don't let her coyness seduce you. ²⁶ For a prostitute will bring a man to poverty, and an adulteress may cost him his very life. ²⁷ Can a man hold fire against his chest and not be burned? ²⁸ Can he walk on hot coals and not blister his feet? ²⁹ So it is with the man who commits adultery with another's wife. He shall not go unpunished for this sin. ³⁰ Excuses might even be found for a thief, if he steals when he is starving! ³¹ But even so, he is fined seven times as much as he stole, though

it may mean selling everything in his house to pay it back.

32 But the man who commits adultery is an utter fool, for he destroys his own soul. 33 Wounds and constant disgrace are his lot, 34 For the woman's husband will be furious in his jealousy, and he will have no mercy on you in his day of vengeance. 35 You won't be able to buy him off no matter what you offer.

It may mean selling everything in his house to pay it back.

But the man who commits adultery is an utter fool, for he destroys his own soul. Wounds and constant disgrace are his lot. For the woman's husband will be furious in his jealousy, and he will have no mercy on you in his day of vengeance. You won't be able to buy him off no matter what you offer.

Psalms for the Seventh Day

31 Lord, I trust in You alone. Don't let my enemies defeat me. Rescue me because You are the God who always does what is right. [2] Answer quickly when I cry to You; bend low and hear my whispered plea. Be for me a great Rock of safety from my foes. [3] Yes, You are my Rock and my fortress; honor Your name by leading me out of this peril. [4] Pull me from the trap my enemies have set for me. For You alone are strong enough. [5, 6] Into Your hand I commit my spirit . . .

You have rescued me, O God who keeps His promises! for I worship only You; and how I hate all those who worship idols, those imitation gods. [7] I am radiant with joy because of Your mercy, for You have listened to my troubles and have seen the crisis in my soul. [8] You have not handed me over to my enemy, but have given me open ground in which to maneuver.

[9, 10] O Lord, have mercy on me in my anguish. My eyes are red from weeping; my health is broken from sorrow. I am pining away with grief; my years are shortened, drained away because of sadness. My sins have sapped my strength; I stoop with sorrow and with shame. [11] I am scorned by all my enemies and even more by my neighbors and friends. They dread meeting me and look the other way when I go by.

¹² I am forgotten like a dead man, like a broken and discarded pot. ¹³ I heard the lies about me, the slanders of my enemies. Everywhere I looked I was afraid, for they were plotting against my life.

¹⁴, ¹⁵ But I was trusting You, O Lord. I said, "You alone are my God; my times are in Your hands. Rescue me from those who hunt me down relentlessly. ¹⁶ Let Your favor shine again upon Your servant; save me just because You are so kind! ¹⁷ Don't disgrace me, Lord, by not replying when I call to You for aid. But let the wicked be shamed by what they trust in; let them lie silently in their graves, ¹⁸ Their lying lips quieted at last — the lips of these arrogant men who are accusing honest men of evil deeds."

¹⁹ Oh, how great is Your goodness to those who publicly declare that You will rescue them. For You have stored up great blessings for those who trust and reverence You.

²⁰ Hide Your loved ones in the shelter of Your presence, safe beneath Your hand, safe from all conspiring men. ²¹ Blessed is the Lord, for He has shown me that His never-failing love protects me like the walls of a fort! ²² I spoke too hastily when I said, "The Lord has deserted me," for You listened to my plea and answered me.

²³ Oh, love the Lord all of you who are His people; for the Lord protects those who are loyal to Him, but harshly punishes all who haughtily reject Him. ²⁴ So cheer up! Take courage if you are depending on the Lord!

32 What happiness for those whose guilt has been forgiven! What joys when sins are covered over! What relief for those who have confessed their sins and God has cleared their record.

3 There was a time when I wouldn't admit what a sinner I was. But my dishonesty made me miserable and filled my days with frustration. 4 All day and all night Your hand was heavy on me. My strength evaporated like water on a sunny day 5 Until I finally admitted all my sins to You and stopped trying to hide them. I said to myself, "I will confess them to the Lord." And You forgave me! All my guilt is gone!

6 After this experience, I say that every believer should confess his sins to God as soon as he becomes aware of them, while there is yet time to be forgiven. If he does this, judgment will not touch him.

7 You are my hiding place from every storm of life; You even keep me from getting into trouble! You surround me with songs of victory. 8 I will instruct you (says the Lord) and guide you along the best pathway for your life; I will advise you and watch your progress. 9 Don't be like a senseless horse or mule that has to have a bit in its mouth to keep it in line!

10 Many sorrows come to the wicked, but abiding love surrounds those who trust in the Lord. 11 So rejoice in Him, all those who are His, and shout for joy, all those who try to obey Him.

33 Let all the joys of the godly well up in praise to the Lord, for it is right to praise Him. 2 Play joyous melodies of praise upon the lyre and on the harp! 3 Compose new songs of praise to Him, accompanied skillfully on the harp; sing joyfully.

4 For all God's words are right, and everything He does is worthy of our trust. 5 He loves whatever is

just and good; the earth is filled with His tender love.
⁶ He merely spoke, and the heavens were formed, and
all the galaxies of stars. ⁷ He made the oceans, pouring them into His vast reservoirs.

⁸ Let everyone in all the world — men, women and
children — fear the Lord and stand in awe of Him.
⁹ For when He but spoke, the world began! It ap-
peared at His command! ¹⁰ And with a breath He
can scatter the plans of all the nations who oppose
Him, ¹¹ But His own plan stands forever. His intentions are the same for every generation.

¹² Blessed is the nation whose God is the Lord,
whose people He has chosen as His own. ¹³, ¹⁴, ¹⁵ The
Lord gazes down upon mankind from heaven where
He lives. He has made their hearts and closely watches
everything they do.

¹⁶, ¹⁷ The best-equipped army cannot save a king
— for great strength is not enough to save anyone. A
war horse is a poor risk for winning victories — it is
strong but it cannot save.

¹⁸, ¹⁹ But the eyes of the Lord are watching over
those who fear Him, who rely upon His steady love.
He will keep them from death even in times of famine!
²⁰ We depend upon the Lord alone to save us. Only
He can help us, He protects us like a shield. ²¹ No
wonder we are happy in the Lord! For we are trusting
Him! We trust His holy name. ²² Yes, Lord, let Your
constant love surround us, for our hopes are in You
alone.

34 I will praise the Lord no matter what happens. I
will constantly speak of His glories and grace. ² I will
boast of all His kindness to me. Let all who are dis-

couraged take heart! ³ Let us praise the Lord together, and exalt His name.

⁴ For I cried to Him and He answered me! He freed me from all my fears. ⁵ Others too were radiant at what He did for them. Theirs was no downcast look of rejection! ⁶ This poor man cried to the Lord — and the Lord heard him and saved him out of his troubles. ⁷ For the Angel of the Lord guards and rescues all who reverence Him.

⁸ Oh, put God to the test and see how kind He is! See for yourself the way His mercies shower down on all who trust in Him! ⁹ If you belong to the Lord, reverence Him; for everyone who does this has everything he needs. ¹⁰ Even strong young lions sometimes go hungry, but those of us who reverence the Lord will never lack any good thing.

¹¹ Sons and daughters, come and listen and let me teach you the importance of trusting and fearing the Lord. ¹² Do you want a long, good life? ¹³ Then watch your tongue! Keep your lips from lying. ¹⁴ Turn from all known sin and spend your time in doing good. Try to live in peace with everyone; work hard at it.

¹⁵ For the eyes of the Lord are intently watching all who live good lives, and He gives attention when they cry to Him. ¹⁶ But the Lord has made up His mind to wipe out even the memory of evil men from the earth. ¹⁷ Yes, the Lord hears the good man when he calls to Him for help, and saves him out of all his troubles.

¹⁸ The Lord is close to those whose hearts are breaking; He rescues those who are humbly sorry for

their sins. [19] The good man does not escape all troubles — he has them too. But the Lord helps him in each and every one. [20] God even protects him from accidents.

[21] Calamity will surely overtake the wicked; heavy penalties are meted out to those who hate the good. [22] But as for those who serve the Lord, He will redeem them; everyone who takes refuge in Him will be freely pardoned.

35 O Lord, fight those fighting me; declare war on them for their attacks on me. [2] Put on Your armor, take Your shield and protect me by standing in front. [3] Lift Your spear in my defense, for my pursuers are getting very close. Let me hear You say that You will save me from them! [4] Dishonor those who are trying to kill me! Turn them back and confuse them. [5] Blow them away like chaff in the wind — wind sent by the Angel of the Lord. [6] Make their path dark and slippery before them, with the Angel of the Lord pursuing them. [7] For though I did them no wrong, yet they laid a trap for me and dug a pitfall in my path. [8] Let them be overtaken by sudden ruin, caught in their own net, and destroyed.

[9] But I will rejoice in the Lord. He shall rescue me! [10] From the bottom of my heart praise rises to Him. Where is His equal in all of heaven and earth? Who else protects the weak and helpless from the strong, and the poor and needy from those who would rob them?

[11] These evil men swear to a lie. They accuse me of things I have never even heard about. [12] I do them good, but they return me harm. I am sinking down to

death. ¹³ When they were ill, I mourned before the Lord in sackcloth, asking Him to make them well; I refused to eat; I prayed for them with utmost earnestness, but God did not listen. ¹⁴ I went about sadly as though it were my mother, friend or brother who was sick and nearing death. ¹⁵ But now that I am in trouble they are glad; they come together in meetings filled with slander against me — I didn't even know some of those who were there. ¹⁶ For they gather with the worthless fellows of the town and spend their time cursing me.

¹⁷ Lord, how long will You stand there, doing nothing? Act now and rescue me, for I have but one life and these young lions are out to get it. ¹⁸ Save me, and I will thank You publicly before the entire congregation, before the largest crowd I can find.

¹⁹ Don't give victory to those who fight me without any reason! Don't let them rejoice at my fall — let them die. ²⁰ They don't talk of peace and doing good, but of plots against innocent men who are minding their own business. ²¹ They shout that they have seen *me* doing wrong! "Aha!" they say, "With our own eyes we saw him do it." ²² Lord, You know all about it. Don't stay silent! Don't desert me now!

²³ Rise up, O Lord my God; vindicate me. ²⁴ Declare me "not guilty," for You are just. Don't let my enemies rejoice over me in my troubles. ²⁵ Don't let them say, "Aha! Our dearest wish against him will soon be fulfilled!" and, "At last we have him!" ²⁶ Shame them; let these who boast against me and who rejoice at my troubles be themselves overcome by misfortune that strips them bare of everything they own. Bare them to dishonor. ²⁷ But give great joy to

all who wish me well. Let them shout with delight,
"Great is the Lord who enjoys helping His child!"
28 And I will tell everyone how great and good You
are; I will praise You all day long.

8 So she seduced him with her pretty speech, her coaxing and her wheedling, until he yielded to her. He couldn't resist her flattery. 22 He followed her as an ox going to the butcher, or as a stag caught, 23 Waiting to be killed with an arrow through its heart. He was as a bird flying into a snare, not knowing the fate awaiting it there.

Listen to me, young men, and not only listen but obey; don't let your desires get out of hand; don't

Proverbs for the Seventh Day

7 Follow my advice, my son; always keep it in mind and stick to it. ² Obey me and live! Guard my words as your most precious possession. ³ Write them down, and also keep them deep within your heart. ⁴ Love wisdom like a sweetheart; make her a beloved member of your family. ⁵ Let her hold you back from visiting a prostitute, from listening to her flattery.

⁶ I was looking out the window of my house one day, ⁷ And saw a simple-minded lad, a young man lacking common sense, ⁸, ⁹ Walking at twilight down the street to the house of this wayward girl, a prostitute. ¹⁰ She approached him, saucy and pert, and dressed seductively. ¹¹, ¹² She was the brash, coarse type, seen often in the streets and markets, soliciting at every corner for men to be her lovers.

¹³ She put her arms around him and kissed him, and with a saucy look she said, ¹⁴ "I've decided to forget our quarrel! ¹⁵ I was just coming to look for you and here you are! ¹⁶, ¹⁷ My bed is spread with lovely, colored sheets of finest linen imported from Egypt, perfumed with myrrh, aloes and cinnamon. ¹⁸ Come on, let's take our fill of love until morning, ¹⁹ For my husband is away on a long trip. ²⁰ He has taken a wallet full of money with him, and won't return for several days."

²¹ So she seduced him with her pretty speech, her coaxing and her wheedling, until he yielded to her. He couldn't resist her flattery. ²² He followed her as an ox going to the butcher, or as a stag that is trapped, ²³ Waiting to be killed with an arrow through its heart. He was as a bird flying into a snare, not knowing the fate awaiting it there.

²⁴ Listen to me, young men, and not only listen but obey. ²⁵ Don't let your desires get out of hand; don't let yourself think about her; don't go near her; stay away from where she walks, lest she tempt you and seduce you. ²⁶ For she has been the ruin of multitudes — a vast host of men have been her victims. ²⁷ If you want to find the road to hell, look for her house.

Psalms for the Eighth Day

36 Sin lurks deep in the hearts of the wicked, forever urging them on to evil deeds. They have no fear of God to hold them back. ² Instead, in their conceit, they think they can hide their evil deeds and not get caught. ³ Everything they say is crooked and deceitful; they are no longer wise and good. ⁴ They lie awake at night to hatch their evil plots, instead of planning how to keep away from wrong.

⁵ Your steadfast love, O Lord, is as great as all the heavens. Your faithfulness reaches beyond the clouds! ⁶ Your justice is as solid as God's mountains. Your decisions are as full of wisdom as the oceans are with water. You are concerned for men and animals alike! ⁷ How precious is Your constant love, O God! All humanity takes refuge in the shadow of Your wings! ⁸ You feed them with blessings from Your own table and let them drink from Your rivers of delight.

⁹ For You are the Fountain of Life; our light is from Your Light. ¹⁰ Pour out Your unfailing love on those who know You! Never stop giving Your salvation to those who long to do Your will.

¹¹ Don't let these proud men trample me. Don't let their wicked hands push me around. ¹² Look! They have fallen. They are thrown down and will not rise again.

37 Never envy the wicked! ² Soon they fade away like grass and disappear. ³ Trust in the Lord instead. Be kind and good to others; then you will live safely here in the land and prosper, feeding in safety.

⁴ Be delighted with the Lord! Then He will give you all your heart's desires. ⁵ Commit everything you do to the Lord. Trust Him to help you do it and He will. ⁶ Your innocence will be clear to everyone. He will vindicate you with the blazing light of justice shining down as from the noonday sun.

⁷ Rest in the Lord; wait patiently for Him to act. Don't be envious of evil men who prosper.

⁸ Stop your anger! Turn off your wrath. Don't fret and worry — it only leads to harm. ⁹ For the wicked shall be destroyed, but those who trust the Lord shall be given every blessing. ¹⁰ Only a little while and the wicked shall disappear. You will look for them in vain. ¹¹ But all who humble themselves before the Lord shall be given every blessing, and shall have wonderful peace.

¹², ¹³ The Lord is laughing at those who plot against the godly, for He knows their judgment day is coming. ¹⁴ Evil men take aim to slay the poor; they are ready to butcher those who do right. ¹⁵ But their swords will be plunged into their own hearts and all their weapons will be broken.

¹⁶ It is better to have little and be godly than to own an evil man's wealth; ¹⁷ For the strength of evil men shall be broken, but the Lord takes care of those He has forgiven.

¹⁸ Day by day the Lord observes the good deeds

done by godly men, and gives them eternal rewards.
[19] He cares for them when times are hard; even in
famine, they will have enough. [20] But evil men shall
perish. These enemies of God will wither like grass,
and disappear like smoke. [21] Evil men borrow and
"cannot pay it back"! But the good man returns what
he owes with some extra besides. [22] Those blessed
by the Lord shall inherit the earth; but those cursed
by Him shall die.

[23] The steps of good men are directed by the Lord.
He delights in each step they take. [24] If they fall it
isn't fatal, for the Lord holds them with His hand.

[25] I have been young and now I am old. And in all
my years I have never seen the Lord forsake a man
who loves Him; nor have I seen the children of the
godly go hungry. [26] Instead, the godly are able to be
generous with their gifts and loans to others, and their
children are a blessing.

[27] So if you want an eternal home, leave your evil,
low-down ways and live good lives. [28] For the Lord
loves justice and fairness; He will never abandon His
people. They will be kept safe forever; but all who
love wickedness shall perish.

[29] The godly shall be firmly planted in the land,
and live there forever. [30, 31] The godly man is a good
counselor because he is just and fair and knows right
from wrong.

[32] Evil men spy on the godly, waiting for an excuse
to accuse them and then demanding their death!
[33] But the Lord will not let these evil men succeed, or
let the godly be condemned when they are brought before the judge.

34 Don't be impatient for the Lord to act! Keep steadily along His pathway and in due season He will honor you with every blessing, and you will see the wicked destroyed. 35, 36 I myself have seen it happen: a proud and evil man, towering like a cedar of Lebanon, but when I looked again, he was gone! I searched but could not find him! 37 But the good man — what a different story! For the good man — the blameless, the upright, the man of peace — he has a wonderful future ahead of him. For him there is a happy ending. 38 But evil men shall be destroyed, and their posterity shall be cut off.

39 The Lord saves the godly! He is their salvation and their refuge when trouble comes. 40 Because they trust in Him, He helps them and delivers them from the plots of evil men.

38 O Lord, don't punish me while You are angry! 2 Your arrows have struck deep; Your blows are crushing me. 3, 4 Because of Your anger my body is sick, my health is broken beneath my sins. They are like a flood, higher than my head; they are a burden too heavy to bear. 5, 6 My wounds are festering and full of pus. Because of my sins I am bent and racked with pain. My days are filled with anguish. 7 My loins burn with inflammation and my whole body is diseased. 8 I am exhausted and crushed; I groan in despair.

9 Lord, You know how I long for my health once more. You hear my every sigh. 10 My heart beats wildly, my strength fails, and I am going blind. 11 My loved ones and friends stay away, fearing my disease. Even my own family stands at a distance.

¹² Meanwhile my enemies are trying to kill me. They plot my ruin and spend all their waking hours planning treachery. ¹³, ¹⁴ But I am deaf to all their threats; I am silent before them as a man who cannot speak. I have nothing to say. ¹⁵ For I am waiting for You, O Lord my God. Come and protect me. ¹⁶ Put an end to their arrogance, these who gloat when I am cast down!

¹⁷ How constantly I find myself upon the verge of sin; this source of sorrow always stares me in the face. ¹⁸ I confess my sins; I am sorry for what I have done. ¹⁹ But my enemies persecute with vigor, and continue to hate me — though I have done nothing against them to deserve it. ²⁰ They repay me evil for good and hate me for standing for the right.

²¹ Don't leave me, Lord! Don't go away! ²² Come quickly! Help me, O my Savior.

39 I said to myself, I'm going to quit complaining! I'll keep quiet, especially when the ungodly are around me. ², ³ But as I stood there silently, the turmoil within me grew to the bursting point. The more I mused, the hotter the fires inside. Then at last I spoke, and pled with God: ⁴ Lord, help me to realize how brief my time on earth will be! Help me to know that I am here for but a moment more. ⁵, ⁶ My life is no longer than my hand! My whole lifetime is but a moment to You. Proud man! Frail as breath! A shadow! And all his busy rushing ends in nothing. He heaps up riches for someone else to spend. ⁷ And so, Lord, my only hope is in You.

⁸ Save me from being overpowered by my sins, for even fools will mock me then.

⁹ Lord, I am speechless before You. I will not open my mouth to speak one word of complaint, for my punishment is from You.

¹⁰ Lord, don't hit me any more — I am exhausted beneath Your hand. ¹¹ When You punish a man for his sins, he is destroyed; for he is as fragile as a moth-infested cloth; yes, man is frail as breath.

¹² Hear my prayer, O Lord; listen to my cry! Don't sit back, unmindful of my tears! For I am Your guest! I am a traveler passing through the earth, as all my fathers were!

¹³ Spare me, Lord! Let me recover and be filled with happiness again before my death.

40 I waited patiently for God to help me; then He listened and heard my cry. ² He lifted me out of the pit of despair, out from the bog and the mire, and set my feet on a hard, firm path and steadied me as I walked along. ³ He has given me a new song to sing, of praises to our God. Now many will hear of the glorious things He did for me, and stand in awe before the Lord, and put their trust in Him. ⁴ Many blessings are given to those who trust the Lord, and have no confidence in those who are proud, or who trust in idols.

⁵ O Lord my God, many and many a time You have done great miracles for us, and we are ever in Your thoughts. Who else can do such glorious things? No one else can be compared with You. There isn't time to tell of all Your wonderful deeds.

⁶ It isn't sacrifices and offerings which You really want from Your people. Burnt animals bring no special joy to Your heart. But You have accepted the

offer of my lifelong service. ⁷ Then I said, "See, I have come, just as all the prophets foretold. ⁸ And I delight to do Your will, my God; for Your law is written upon My heart!"

⁹ I have told everyone the Good News that You forgive men's sins. I have not been timid about it, as You well know, O Lord. ¹⁰ I have not kept this Good News hidden in my heart, but have proclaimed Your lovingkindness and truth to all the congregation.

¹¹ O Lord, don't hold back Your tender mercies from me! My only hope is in Your love and faithfulness! ¹² Otherwise I perish, for problems far too big for me to solve are piled higher than my head. Meanwhile my sins, too many to count, have all caught up with me and I am ashamed to look up. My heart quails within me.

¹³ Please, Lord, rescue me! Quick! Come and help me! ¹⁴, ¹⁵ Confuse them! Turn them around and send them sprawling — all these who are trying to destroy me. Disgrace these scoffers with their utter failure!

¹⁶ But may the joy of the Lord be given to everyone who loves Him and His salvation. May they constantly exclaim, "How great God is!"

¹⁷ I am poor and needy, yet the Lord is thinking about me right now! O my God, You are my helper; You are my Savior; come quickly, and save me. Please don't delay!

Proverbs for the Eighth Day

8 Can't you hear the voice of wisdom? She is standing at the city gates and at every fork in the road, and at the door of every house. Listen to what she says: [4, 5] "Listen, men!" she calls. "How foolish and naive you are! Let me give you understanding. O foolish ones, let me show you common sense! [6, 7] Listen to me! For I have important information for you. Everything I say is right and true, for I hate lies and every kind of deception. [8] My advice is wholesome and good. There is nothing of evil in it. [9] My words are plain and clear to anyone with half a mind — if it is only open! [10] My instruction is far more valuable than silver or gold."

[11] For the value of wisdom is far above rubies; nothing can be compared with it. [12] Wisdom and good judgment live together, for wisdom knows where to discover knowledge and understanding. [13] If anyone respects and fears God, he will hate evil. For wisdom hates pride, arrogance, corruption and deceit of every kind.

[14, 15] "I, Wisdom, give good advice and common sense. Because of my strength, kings reign in power. I show the judges who is right and who is wrong. [16] Rulers rule well with my help. [17] I love all who love me. Those who search for me shall surely find

me. [18] Unending riches, honor, justice and righteousness are mine to distribute. [19] My gifts are better than the purest gold or sterling silver! [20] My paths are those of justice and right. [21] Those who love and follow me are indeed wealthy. I fill their treasuries. [22] The Lord formed me in the beginning, before He created anything else. [23] From ages past, I am. I existed before the earth began. [24] I lived before the oceans were created, before the springs bubbled forth their waters onto the earth; [25] Before the mountains and the hills were made. [26] Yes, I was born before God made the earth and fields, and high plateaus.

[27-29] I was there when He established the heavens and formed the great springs in the depths of the oceans. I was there when He set the limits of the seas and gave them His instructions not to spread beyond their boundaries. I was there when He made the blueprint for the earth and oceans. [30] I was always at His side like a little child. I was His constant delight, laughing and playing in His presence. [31] And how happy I was with what He created — His wide world and all His family of mankind! [32] And so, young men, listen to me, for how happy are all who follow my instructions.

[33] Listen to my counsel — oh, don't refuse it — and be wise. [34] Happy is the man who is so anxious to be with me that he watches for me daily at my gates, or waits for me outside my home! [35] For whoever finds me finds Life and wins approval from the Lord. [36] But the one who misses me has injured himself irreparably. Those who refuse me show that they love death."

Psalms for the Ninth Day

41 God blesses those who are kind to the poor. He helps them out of their troubles! ² He protects them and keeps them alive; He publicly honors them and destroys the power of their enemies. ³ He nurses them when they are sick, and soothes their pains and worries.

⁴ "O Lord," I prayed, "be kind and heal me, for I have confessed my sins." ⁵ But my enemies say, "May he soon die and be forgotten!" ⁶ They act so friendly when they come to visit me while I am sick; but all the time they hate me and are glad that I am lying there upon my bed of pain. And when they leave, they laugh and mock. ⁷ They whisper together about what they will do when I am dead. ⁸ "It's fatal, whatever it is," they say. "He'll never get out of that bed!"

⁹ Even my best friend has turned against me — a man I completely trusted; how often we ate together. ¹⁰ Lord, don't You desert me! Be gracious, Lord, and make me well again so I can pay them back! ¹¹ I know You are pleased with me because You haven't let my enemies triumph over me. ¹² You have preserved me because I was honest; You have admitted me forever to Your presence.

[13] Bless the Lord, the God of Israel, who exists from everlasting ages past — and on into everlasting eternity ahead. Amen and Amen!

42 As the deer pants for water, so I long for You, O God. [2] I thirst for God, the living God. Where can I find Him to come and stand before Him? [3] Day and night I weep for His help, and all the while my enemies taunt me. "Where is this God of yours?" they scoff.

[4, 5] Take courage, my soul! Do you remember those times (but how could you ever forget them!) when you led a great procession to the Temple on festival days, singing with joy, praising the Lord? Why then be downcast? Why be discouraged and sad? Hope in God! I shall yet praise Him again! Yes, I shall again praise Him for His help. [6] Yet I am standing here depressed and gloomy; but I will meditate upon Your kindness to this lovely land where the Jordan River flows and where Mount Hermon and Mount Mizar stand. [7] All your waves and billows have gone over me, and floods of sorrow pour upon me like a thundering cataract.

[8] Yet day by day the Lord also pours out His steadfast love upon me, and through the night I sing His songs and pray to God who gives me life.

[9] "O God my Rock," I cry, "why have You forsaken me? Why must I suffer these attacks from my enemies?" [10] Their taunts pierce me like a fatal wound; again and again they scoff, "Where is that God of yours?" [11] But O my soul, don't be discouraged! Don't be upset! Expect God to act! For I know that I shall again have plenty of reason to praise Him for all that He will do! He is my help! He is my God!

43 O God, defend me from the charges of these merciless, deceitful men. ² For You are God, my only place of refuge. Why have You tossed me aside? Why must I mourn at the oppression of my enemies?

³ Oh, send out Your light and Your truth — let them lead me. Let them lead me to Your Temple on Your holy mountain, Zion. ⁴ There I will go to the altar of God my exceeding joy, and praise Him with my harp. O God — my God! ⁵ O my soul, why be so gloomy and discouraged? Trust in God! I shall again praise Him for His wondrous help; He will make me smile again, *for He is my God!*

44 O God, we have heard of the glorious miracles You did in the days of long ago. Our forefathers have told us how You drove the heathen nations from this land and gave it all to us, spreading Israel from one end of the country to the other. ³ They did not conquer by their own strength and skill; but by Your mighty power and because You smiled upon them and favored them.

⁴ You are my King and my God. Decree victories for Your people! ⁵ For it is only by Your power and through Your name that we tread down our enemies; ⁶ I do not trust my weapons! They could never save me. ⁷ Only You can give us the victory over those who hate us.

⁸ My constant boast is God. I can never thank You enough! ⁹ And yet for a time, O Lord, You have tossed us aside in dishonor, and have not helped us in our battles. ¹⁰ You have actually fought against us and defeated us before our foes. Our enemies have invaded our land and pillaged the countryside.

¹¹ You have treated us like sheep in a slaughter pen, and scattered us among the nations. ¹² You sold us for a pittance. You valued us at nothing at all. ¹³ The neighboring nations laugh and mock at us because of all the evil You have sent. ¹⁴ You have made the word "Jew" a byword of contempt and shame among the nations, disliked by all. ¹⁵, ¹⁶ I am constantly despised, mocked, taunted and cursed by my vengeful enemies.

¹⁷ And all this has happened, Lord, despite our loyalty to You. We have not violated Your covenant. ¹⁸ Our hearts have not deserted You! We have not left Your path by a single step. ¹⁹ If we had, we could understand Your punishing us in the barren wilderness and sending us into darkness and death. ²⁰ If we had turned away from worshiping our God, and were worshiping idols, ²¹ Would God not know it? Yes, He knows the secrets of every heart. ²² But that is not our case! For we are facing death threats constantly because of serving You! We are like sheep awaiting slaughter.

²³Waken! Rouse Yourself! Don't sleep, O Lord! Are we cast off forever? ²⁴ Why do You look the other way? Why do You ignore our sorrows and oppression? ²⁵ We lie face downward in the dust. ²⁶ Rise up, O Lord, and come and help us. Save us by Your constant love.

45 My heart is overflowing with a beautiful thought! I will write a lovely poem to the King, for I am as full of words as the speediest writer pouring out his story.

² You are the fairest of all;
Your words are filled with grace;

God Himself is blessing You forever!
3 Arm Yourself, O Mighty One,
  So glorious, so majestic!
4 And in Your majesty
  Go on to victory,
  Defending truth, humility, and justice.
  Go forth to awe-inspiring deeds!
5 Your arrows are sharp
  In Your enemies' hearts;
  They fall before You.
6 Your throne, O God, endures forever.
  Justice is Your royal scepter.
7 You love what is good
  And hate what is wrong.
  Therefore God, Your God,
  Has given You more gladness
  Than anyone else.

8 Your robes are perfumed with myrrh, aloes and
cassia. In your inlaid palaces of ivory, lovely music is
being played for your enjoyment. 9 Kings' daughters
are among your concubines. Standing beside you is
the queen, wearing jewelry of finest gold from Ophir.
10, 11 "I advise you, O daughter, not to fret about
your parents in your homeland far away. Your royal
husband delights in your beauty. Reverence him, for
he is your lord. 12 The people of Tyre, the richest
people of our day, will shower you with gifts and en-
treat your favors."

13 The bride, a princess, waits within her chamber,
robed in beautiful clothing woven with gold. 14 Lovely she is, led beside her maids of honor to the king!
15 What a joyful, glad procession as they enter in the
palace gates! 16 "Your sons will some day be kings

like their father. They shall sit on thrones around the world!

¹⁷ I will cause your name to be honored in all generations; the nations of the earth will praise you forever."

Proverbs for the Ninth Day

9 Wisdom has built a palace supported on seven pillars, ² And has prepared a great banquet, and mixed the wines, ³ And sent out her maidens inviting all to come. She calls from the busiest intersections in the city, ⁴ "Come, you simple ones without good judgment; ⁵ Come to wisdom's banquet and drink the wines that I have mixed. ⁶ Leave behind your foolishness and begin to live; learn how to be wise."

⁷, ⁸ If you rebuke a mocker, you will only get a smart retort; yes, he will snarl at you. So don't bother with him; he will only hate you for trying to help him. But a wise man, when rebuked, will love you all the more. ⁹ Teach a wise man, and he will be the wiser; teach a good man, and he will learn more; ¹⁰ *For the reverence and fear of God are basic to all wisdom. Knowing God results in every other kind of understanding.* ¹¹ I, Wisdom, will make the hours of your day more profitable and the years of your life more fruitful. ¹² Wisdom is its own reward, and if you scorn her, you hurt only yourself.

¹³ A prostitute is loud and brash, and never has enough of lust and shame. ¹⁴ She sits at the door of her house or stands at the street corners of the city, ¹⁵ Whispering to men going by, and to those minding their own business. ¹⁶ "Come home with me," she

urges simpletons, [17] "Stolen melons are the sweetest; stolen apples taste the best!" [18] But they don't realize that her former guests are now citizens of hell.

Psalms for the Tenth Day

46 God is our refuge and strength, a tested help in times of trouble. ² And so we need not fear even if the world blows up, and the mountains crumble into the sea. ³ Let the oceans roar and foam; let the mountains tremble!

⁴ There is a river of joy flowing through the City of our God — the sacred home of the God above all gods. ⁵ God Himself is living in that City; therefore it stands unmoved despite the turmoil everywhere. He will not delay His help. ⁶ The nations rant and rave in anger — but when God speaks, the earth melts in submission and kingdoms totter into ruin.

⁷ The Commander of the armies of heaven is here among us. He, the God of Jacob, has come to rescue us. ⁸ Come, see the glorious things that our God does, how He brings ruin upon the world, ⁹ And causes wars to end throughout the earth, breaking and burning every weapon. ¹⁰ "Stand silent! Know that I am God! I shall be honored by every nation in the world!"

¹¹ The Commander of the heavenly armies is here among *us!* He, the God of Jacob, has come to rescue *us!*

47 Come everyone, and clap for joy! Shout triumphant praises to the Lord! ² For the Lord, the God above all gods, is awesome beyond words; He is the great King of all the earth. ³ He subdues the nations before us, ⁴ And will personally select His choicest blessings for His Jewish people — the very best for those He loves.

⁵ God has ascended (into heaven) with a mighty shout, with trumpets blaring. ⁶, ⁷ Sing out your praises to our God, our King. Yes, sing your highest praises to our King, the King of all the earth. Sing thoughtful praises! ⁸ He reigns above the nations, sitting on His holy throne. ⁹ The Gentile rulers of the world have joined with us in praising Him — praising the God of Abraham — for the battle shields of all the armies of the world are His trophies. He is highly honored everywhere.

48 How great is the Lord! How much we should praise Him. He lives upon Mount Zion in Jerusalem. ² What a glorious sight! See Mount Zion rising north of the city high above the plains for all to see — Mount Zion, joy of all the earth, the residence of the great King.

³ God Himself is the defender of Jerusalem. ⁴ The kings of the earth have arrived together to inspect the city. ⁵ They marvel at the sight and hurry home again, ⁶ Afraid of what they have seen; they are filled with panic like a woman in travail! ⁷ For God destroys the mightiest warships with a breath of wind! ⁸ We have heard of the city's glory — the city of our God, the Commander of the armies of heaven. And now we see it for ourselves! God has established Jerusalem forever.

⁹ Lord, here in Your Temple we meditate upon Your kindness and Your love. ¹⁰ Your name is known throughout the earth, O God. You are praised everywhere for the salvation You have scattered throughout the world. ¹¹ O Jerusalem, rejoice! O people of Judah, rejoice! For God will see to it that you are finally treated fairly. ¹² Go, inspect the city! Walk around and count her many towers! ¹³ Note her walls and tour her palaces, so that you can tell your children!

¹⁴ For this great God is our God forever and ever. He will be our guide until we die.

49 Listen everyone! High and low, rich and poor, all around the world — listen to my words, ³ For they are wise and filled with insight.

⁴ I will tell in song accompanied by harps the answer to one of life's most perplexing problems: ⁵ *There is no need to fear when times of trouble come,* even though surrounded by enemies! ⁶ For they trust in their wealth and boast about how rich they are! ⁷ Yet not one of them, though rich as kings, can ransome his own brother from the penalty of sin! For God's forgiveness does not come that way! ⁸, ⁹ For a soul is far too precious to be ransomed by mere earthly wealth. There is not enough of it in all the earth to buy eternal life for just one soul, to keep it out of hell.

¹⁰ Rich man! Proud man! Wise man! You must die like all the rest! You have no greater lease on life than foolish, stupid men. You must leave your wealth to others! ¹¹ You name your estates after yourselves as though your lands could be forever yours, and you could live on them eternally! ¹² But man with all his

pomp must die like any animal! [13] Such is the folly of these men, though after they die they will be quoted as having great wisdom!

[14] Death is the shepherd of all mankind. And "in the morning" those who are evil will be the slaves of those who are good. For the power of their wealth is gone when they die; they cannot take it with them.

[15] But as for me, God will redeem my soul from the power of death, for He will receive me. [16] So do not be dismayed when evil men grow rich and build their lovely homes. [17] For when they die they carry nothing with them! Their honors will not follow them. [18] Though a man calls himself happy all through his life — and the world loudly applauds success — [19] Yet in the end he dies like everyone else, and enters eternal darkness.

[20] For man with all his pomp must die like any animal!

50 The mighty God, the Lord, has summoned all mankind from east to west!

[2] God's glory-light shines from the beautiful Temple on Mount Zion. [3] He comes with the noise of thunder, surrounded by devastating fire; a great storm rages round about Him. [4] He has come to judge His people. To heaven and earth He shouts, [5] "Gather together My own people who by their sacrifice upon My altar have promised to obey Me." [6] God will judge them with complete fairness, for all heaven declares that He is just.

[7] O My people, listen! For I am your God. Listen! Here are My charges against you: [8] I have no com-

plaint about the sacrifices you bring to My altar, for you bring them regularly. 9 But it isn't sacrificial bullocks and goats that I really want from you! 10, 11 For all the animals of field and forest are Mine! The cattle on a thousand hills! And all the birds upon the mountains! 12 If I were hungry, I would not mention it to you — for all the world is Mine, and everything in it. 13 No, I don't need your sacrifices of flesh and blood! 14, 15 What I want from you is your true thanks; I want your promises fulfilled. *I want you to trust Me in your times of trouble, so I can rescue you, and you can give Me glory!*

16 But God says to evil men: Recite My laws no longer, and stop claiming My promises, 17 For you have refused My discipline, disregarding My laws. 18 You see a thief and help him, and spend your time with evil and immoral men. 19 You curse and lie, and vile language streams from your mouths. 20 You slander your own brother. 21 I remained silent — you thought I didn't care — but now your time of punishment has come, and I list all the above charges against you. 22 This is the last chance, for all of you who have forgotten God before I tear you apart — and no one can help then.

23 But true praise is a worthy sacrifice; this really honors Me. Those who walk My paths will receive salvation from the Lord.

Proverbs for the Tenth Day

These are the proverbs of Solomon:

10 Happy is the man with a level-headed son; sad the mother of a rebel. ² Ill-gotten gain brings no lasting happiness; right living does. ³ The Lord will not let a good man starve to death, nor will He let the wicked man's riches continue forever. ⁴ Lazy men are soon poor; hard workers get rich. ⁵ A wise youth makes hay while the sun shines, but what a shame to see a lad who sleeps away his hour of opportunity. ⁶ The good man is covered with blessings from head to foot, but an evil man inwardly curses his luck. ⁷ We all have happy memories of good men gone to their reward, but the names of wicked men stink after them. ⁸ The wise man is glad to be instructed, but a self-sufficient fool falls flat on his face. ⁹ A good man has firm footing, but a crook will slip and fall. ¹⁰ Winking at sin leads to sorrow; bold reproof leads to peace. ¹¹ There is living truth in what a good man says, but the mouth of the evil man is filled with curses. ¹² Hatred stirs old quarrels, but love overlooks insults. ¹³ Men with common sense are admired as counselors; those without it are beaten as servants. ¹⁴ A wise man holds his tongue. Only a fool blurts out everything he knows; that only leads to sorrow and trouble. ¹⁵ The rich man's wealth is his only strength. The poor man's poverty is his only

curse. 16 The good man's earnings advance the cause
of righteousness. The evil man squanders his on sin.
17 Anyone willing to be corrected is on the pathway
to life. Anyone refusing has lost his chance. 18 To
hate is to be a liar; to slander is to be a fool. 19 Don't
talk so much. You keep putting your foot in your
mouth. Be sensible and turn off the flow! 20 When a
good man speaks, he is worth listening to, but the
words of fools are a dime a dozen. 21 A godly man
gives good advice, but a rebel is destroyed by lack of
common sense. 22 The Lord's blessing is our greatest
wealth. All our work adds nothing to it! 23 A fool's
fun is being bad; a wise man's fun is being wise!
24 The wicked man's fears will all come true, and so
will the good man's hopes. 25 Disaster strikes like a
cyclone and the wicked are whirled away. But the
good man has a strong anchor. 26 A lazy fellow is a
pain to his employers—like smoke in their eyes or
vinegar that sets the teeth on edge. 27 Reverence for
God adds hours to each day; so how can the wicked
expect a long, good life? 28 The hope of good men is
eternal happiness; the hopes of evil men are all in vain.
29 God protects the upright but destroys the wicked.
30 The good shall never lose God's blessings, but the
wicked shall lose everything. 31 The good man gives
wise advice, but the liar's counsel is shunned. 32 The
upright speak what is helpful; the wicked speak
rebellion.

Psalms for the Eleventh Day

(Written after Nathan the prophet had come to inform David of God's judgment against him because of his adultery with Bathsheba, and his murder of Uriah, her husband.)

51 O loving and kind God, have mercy. Have pity upon me and take away the awful stain of my transgressions. ² Oh, wash me, cleanse me from this guilt. Let me be pure again. ³ For I admit my shameful deed — it haunts me day and night. ⁴ It is against You and You alone I sinned, and did this terrible thing. You saw it all, and Your sentence against me is just. ⁵ But I was born a sinner, yes, from the moment my mother conceived me. ⁶ You deserve honesty from the heart; yes, utter sincerity and truthfulness. Oh, give me this wisdom.

⁷ Sprinkle me with the cleansing blood and I shall be clean again. Wash me and I shall be whiter than snow. ⁸ And after You have punished me, give me back my joy again. ⁹ Don't keep looking at my sins — erase them from Your sight. ¹⁰ Create in me a new, clean heart, O God, filled with clean thoughts and right desires. ¹¹ Don't toss me aside, banished forever from Your presence. Don't take Your Holy Spirit from me. ¹² Restore to me again the joy of Your salvation, and make me willing to obey You. ¹³ Then I will teach

Your ways to other sinners, and they — guilty like me — will repent and return to You. [14, 15] Don't sentence me to death. O my God, You alone can rescue me. Then I will sing of Your forgiveness, for my lips will be unsealed — oh, how I will praise You.

[16] You don't want penance; if You did, how gladly I would do it! You aren't interested in offerings burned before You on the altar. [17] It is a broken spirit You want — remorse and penitence. A broken and a contrite heart, O God, You will not ignore.

[18] And Lord, don't punish Israel for my sins — help Your people and protect Jerusalem.

[19] And when my heart is right, then You will rejoice in the good that I do and in the bullocks I bring to sacrifice upon Your altar.

Written by David to protest against his enemy Doeg (1 Samuel 22), who later slaughtered 85 priests and their families.

52 You call yourself a *hero*, do you? You *boast* about this evil deed of yours against God's people. [2] You are sharp as a tack in plotting your evil tricks. [3] How you love wickedness — far more than good! And lying more than truth! [4] You love to slander — you love to say anything that will do harm, O man with the lying tongue!

[5] But God will strike you down and pull you from your home, and drag you away from the land of the living. [6] The followers of God will see it happen. They will watch in awe. Then they will laugh and say, [7] "See what happens to those who despise God and trust in their wealth, and become ever more bold in their wickedness."

⁸ But I am like a sheltered olive tree protected by the Lord Himself. I trust in the mercy of God forever and ever. ⁹ O Lord, I will praise You forever and ever for Your punishment. And I will wait for Your mercies — for everyone knows what a merciful God You are.

53 Only a fool would say to himself, "There is no God." And why does he say it? Because of his wicked heart, his dark and evil deeds. His life is corroded with sin.

² God looks down from heaven, searching among all mankind to see if there is a single one who does right and really seeks for God. ³ But all have turned their backs on Him; they are filthy with sin — corrupt and rotten through and through. Not one is good, not one! ⁴ How can this be? Can't they understand anything? For they devour My people like bread and refuse to come to God. ⁵ But soon unheard-of terror will fall on them. God will scatter the bones of these, your enemies! They are doomed, for God has rejected them.

⁶ Oh, that God would come from Zion now and save Israel! Only when the Lord Himself restores them can they ever be really happy again.

Written by David at the time the men of Ziph tried to betray him to Saul.

54 Come with great power, O God, and save me! Defend me with Your might! ² Oh, listen to my prayer. ³ For violent men have risen against me — ruthless men who care nothing for God are seeking my life.

⁴ But God is my helper! He is a friend of mine! ⁵ He will cause the evil deeds of my enemies to boomerang upon them. Do as You promised and put an end to these wicked men, O God. ⁶ Gladly I bring my sacrifices to You; I will praise Your name, O Lord, for it is good.

⁷ God has rescued me from all my trouble, and triumphed over my enemies.

55 Listen to my prayer, O God; don't hide Yourself when I cry to You! ² Hear me, Lord! Listen to me! For I groan and weep beneath my woe.

³ My enemies shout against me and threaten me with death. They surround with terror and plot to kill me. Their fury and hatred rise to engulf me. ⁴ My heart is in anguish within me. Stark fear overpowers me. ⁵ Trembling and horror overwhelm me. ⁶ Oh, for wings like a dove, to fly away and rest! ⁷ I would fly to the far off deserts and stay there. ⁸ I would flee to some refuge from all this storm.

⁹ O Lord, make these enemies begin to quarrel among themselves — destroy them with their own violence and strife. ¹⁰ Though they patrol their walls night and day against invaders, their real problem is internal — wickedness and dishonesty are entrenched in the heart of the city. ¹¹ There is murder and robbery there, and cheating in the markets and everywhere one looks.

¹² It was not an enemy who taunted me — then I could have borne it; I could have hidden and escaped. ¹³ But it was you, a man like myself, my companion and my friend. ¹⁴ What fellowship we had, what won-

derful discussions as we walked together to the Temple of the Lord on holy days.

¹⁵ Let death seize them and cut them down in their prime, for there is sin in their homes, and they are polluted to the depths of their souls. ¹⁶ But I will call upon the Lord to save me — and He will. ¹⁷ I will pray morning, noon and night pleading aloud with God; and He will hear and answer. ¹⁸ Though the tide of battle runs strongly against me, for so many are fighting me, yet He will rescue me. ¹⁹ God Himself — God from everlasting ages past — will answer them! For they refuse to fear Him or even honor His commands.

²⁰ This friend of mine betrayed me — I who was at peace with him. He broke his promises ²¹ His words were oily smooth, but in his heart was war. His words were sweet, but underneath were daggers.

²² Give your burdens to the Lord. He will carry them. He will not permit the godly to slip or fall. ²³ He will send my enemies to the pit of destruction. Murderers and liars will not live out half their days. But I am trusting You to save me.

Proverbs for the Eleventh Day

11 The Lord hates cheating and delights in honesty.

†

² Proud men end in shame, but the meek become wise.

†

³ A good man is guided by his honesty; the evil man is destroyed by his dishonesty.

†

⁴ Your riches won't help you on Judgment Day; only righteousness counts then.

†

⁵ The upright are directed by their honesty; the wicked shall fall beneath their load of sins.

†

⁶ The good man's goodness delivers him; the evil man's treachery is his undoing.

†

⁷ When an evil man dies, his hopes all perish, for they are based upon this earthly life.

†

⁸ God rescues good men from danger while letting the wicked fall into it.

†

⁹ Evil words destroy. Godly skill rebuilds.

¹⁰ The whole city celebrates a good man's success — and also the godless man's death.

†

¹¹ The good influence of godly citizens causes a city to prosper, but the moral decay of the wicked drives it downhill.

†

¹² To quarrel with a neighbor is foolish; a man with good sense holds his tongue.

†

¹³ A gossip goes around spreading rumors, while a trustworthy man tries to quiet them.

†

¹⁴ Without wise leadership, a nation is in trouble; but with good counselors there is safety.

†

¹⁵ Be sure you know a person well before you vouch for his credit! Better refuse than suffer later.

†

¹⁶ Honor goes to kind and gracious women, mere money to cruel men.

†

¹⁷ Your own soul is nourished when you are kind; it is destroyed when you are cruel.

†

¹⁸ The evil man gets rich for the moment, but the good man's reward lasts forever.

†

¹⁹ The good man finds Life; the evil man, Death.

†

²⁰ The Lord hates the stubborn but delights in those who are good.

†

²¹ You can be very sure that the evil man will not

go unpunished forever. And you can also be very sure that God will rescue the children of the godly.

†

22 A beautiful woman lacking discretion and modesty is like a fine gold ring in a pig's snout.

†

23 The good man can look forward to happiness, while the wicked can expect only wrath.

†

24, 25 It is possible to give away and become richer! It is also possible to hold on too tightly and lose everything. Yes, the liberal man shall be rich! By watering others, he waters himself.

†

26 People curse the man who holds his grain for higher prices, but they bless the man who sells it to them in their time of need.

†

27 If you search for good you will find God's favor; if you search for evil you will find His curse.

†

28 Trust in your money and down you go! Trust in God and flourish as a tree!

†

29 The fool who provokes his family to anger and resentment will finally have nothing worthwhile left. He shall be the servant of a wiser man.

†

30 Godly men are growing a tree that bears life-giving fruit, and all who win souls are wise.

†

31 Even the godly shall be rewarded here on earth; how much more the wicked!

Psalms for the Twelfth Day

56 Lord, have mercy on me; all day long the enemy troops press in. So many are proud to fight against me; how they long to conquer me.

³, ⁴ But when I am afraid, I will put my confidence in You. Yes, I will trust the promises of God. And since I am trusting Him, what can mere man do to me? ⁵ They are always twisting what I say. All their thoughts are how to harm me. ⁶ They meet together to perfect their plans; they hide beside the trail, listening for my steps, waiting to kill me. ⁷ They expect to get away with it. Don't let them, Lord. In anger cast them to the ground.

⁸ You have seen me tossing and turning through the night. You have collected all my tears and preserved them in Your bottle! You have recorded every one in Your book.

⁹ The very day I call for help, the tide of battle turns! My enemies flee! This one thing I *know: God is for me!* ¹⁰, ¹¹ I am trusting God — oh, praise His promises! I am not afraid of anything mere man can do to me! Yes, praise His promises. ¹² I will surely do what I have promised, Lord, and thank You for Your help. ¹³ For You have saved me from death and

my feet from slipping, so that I can walk before the Lord in the land of the living.

57   O God, have pity, for I am trusting You! I will hide beneath the shadow of Your wings until this storm is past. ² I will cry to the God of heaven who does such wonders for me. ³ He will send down help from heaven to save me, because of His love and His faithfulness. He will rescue me from these liars who are so intent upon destroying me. ⁴ I am surrounded by fierce lions — hotheads whose teeth are sharp as spears and arrows. Their tongues are like swords. ⁵ Lord, be exalted above the highest heavens! Show Your glory high above the earth. ⁶ My enemies have set a trap for me. Frantic fear grips me. They have dug a pitfall in my path. But look! They themselves have fallen into it!

⁷ O God, my heart is quiet and confident. No wonder I can sing Your praises! ⁸ Rouse yourself, my soul! Arise, O harp and lyre! Let us greet the dawn with song! ⁹ I will thank You publicly throughout the land. I will sing Your praises among the nations. ¹⁰ Your kindness and love are as vast as the heavens. Your faithfulness is higher than the skies.

¹¹ Yes, be exalted, O God, above the heavens. May Your glory shine throughout the earth.

58   Justice? You high and mighty politicians don't even know the meaning of the word! Fairness? Which of you has any left? Not one! All your dealings are crooked: you give "justice" in exchange for bribes. ³ These men are born sinners, lying from their earliest words! ⁴, ⁵ They are poisonous as deadly snakes, cobras that close their ears to the most expert of charmers.

⁶ O God, break off their fangs. Tear out the teeth of these young lions, Lord. ⁷ Let them disappear like water into thirsty ground. Make their weapons useless in their hands. ⁸ Let them be as snails that dissolve into slime; and as those who die at birth, who never see the sun. ⁹ God will sweep away both old and young. He will destroy them more quickly than a cooking pot can feel the blazing fire of thorns beneath it.

¹⁰ The godly shall rejoice in the triumph of right; they shall walk the blood-stained fields of slaughtered, wicked men. ¹¹ Then at last everyone will know that good is rewarded, and that there is a God who judges justly here on earth.

(Written by David at the time King Saul set guards at his home to capture and kill him. 1 Samuel 19:11)

59 O my God, save me from my enemies. Protect me from these who have come to destroy me. ² Preserve me from these criminals, these murderers. ³ They lurk in ambush for my life. Strong men are out there waiting. And not, O Lord, because I've done them wrong. ⁴ Yet they prepare to kill me. Lord, waken! See what is happening! Help me! ⁵ (And O Jehovah, God of heaven's armies, God of Israel, arise and punish the heathen nations surrounding us.) Do not spare these evil, treacherous men. ⁶ At evening they come to spy, slinking around like dogs that prowl the city. ⁷ I hear them shouting insults and cursing God, for "No one will hear us," they think. ⁸ Lord, laugh at them! (And scoff at these surrounding nations too.)

⁹ O God my Strength! I will sing Your praises, for

You are my place of safety. [10] My God is changeless in His love for me and He will come and help me. He will let me see my wish come true upon my enemies. [11] Don't kill them — for my people soon forget such lessons — but stagger them with your power and bring them to their knees. Bring them to the dust, O Lord our shield. [12, 13] They are proud, cursing liars. Angrily destroy them. Wipe them out. (And let the nations find out too that God rules in Israel and will reign throughout the world.) [14, 15] Let these evil men slink back at evening, and prowl the city all night before they are satisfied, howling like dogs and searching for food.

[16] But as for me, I will sing each morning about Your power and mercy. For You have been my high tower of refuge, a place of safety in the day of my distress. [17] O my Strength, to You I sing my praises; for You are my high tower of safety, my God of mercy.

(Written by David at the time he was at war with Syria, with the outcome still uncertain; this was when Joab, captain of his forces, slaughtered 12,000 men of Edom in the Valley of Salt.)

60 O God, You have rejected us and broken our defenses; You have become angry and deserted us. Lord, restore us again to Your favor. [2] You have caused this nation to tremble in fear; You have torn it apart. Lord, heal it now, for it is shaken to its depths. [3] You have been very hard on us and made us reel beneath Your blows.

[4, 5] But You have given us a banner to rally to; all who love truth will rally to it; then You can deliver Your beloved people. Use Your strong right arm to rescue us! [6, 7] God has promised to help us! He has

vowed it by His holiness! No wonder I exult! "Shechem, Succoth, Gilead, Manasseh — still are Mine!" He says. "Judah shall continue to produce kings, and Ephraim great warriors. 8 Moab shall become My lowly servant, and Edom My slave. And I will shout in triumph over the Philistines."

9, 10 Who will bring me in triumph into Edom's strong cities? God will! He who cast us off! He who abandoned us to our foes! 11 Yes, Lord, help us against our enemies, for man's help is useless.

12 With God's help we shall do mighty things, for He will trample down our foes.

Proverbs for the Twelfth Day

12 To learn, you must want to be taught. To refuse reproof is stupid.

†

² The Lord blesses good men and condemns the wicked.

†

³ Wickedness never brings real success; only the godly have that.

†

⁴ A worthy wife is her husband's joy and crown; the other kind corrodes his strength and tears down everything he does.

†

⁵ A good man's mind is filled with honest thoughts; an evil man's mind is crammed with lies.

†

⁶ The wicked accuse; the godly defend.

†

⁷ The wicked shall perish; the godly shall stand.

†

⁸ Everyone admires a man with good sense, but a man with a warped mind is despised.

†

⁹ It is better to get your hands dirty — and eat — than to be too proud to work, and starve.

¹⁰ A good man is concerned for the welfare of his animals, but even the kindness of godless men is cruel.

†

¹¹ Hard work means prosperity; only a fool idles away his time.

†

¹² Crooks are jealous of each other's loot, while good men long to help each other.

†

¹³ Lies will get any man into trouble, but honesty is its own defense.

†

¹⁴ Telling the truth gives a man great satisfaction, and hard work returns many blessings to him.

†

¹⁵ A fool thinks he needs no advice, but a wise man listens to others.

†

¹⁶ A fool is quick-tempered; a wise man stays cool when insulted.

†

¹⁷ A good man is known by his truthfulness; a false man by deceit and lies.

†

¹⁸ Some people like to make cutting remarks, but the words of the wise soothe and heal.

†

¹⁹ Truth stands the test of time; lies are soon exposed.

†

²⁰ Deceit fills hearts that are plotting for evil; joy fills hearts that are planning for good!

†

²¹ No real harm befalls the good, but there is constant trouble for the wicked.

²² God loves those who keep their promises, and hates those who don't.

†

²³ A wise man doesn't display his knowledge, but a fool displays his foolishness.

†

²⁴ Work harder and become a leader; be lazy and never succeed.

†

²⁵ Anxious hearts are very heavy but a word of encouragement does wonders!

†

²⁶ The good man asks advice from friends; the wicked plunge ahead — and fall.

†

²⁷ A lazy man won't even dress the game he gets while hunting, but the diligent man makes good use of everything he finds.

†

²⁸ The path of the godly leads to Life. So why fear Death?

God loves those who keep their promises, and hates those who don't.

A wise man doesn't display his knowledge, but a fool displays his foolishness.

Work harder and become a leader; be lazy and never succeed.

Anxious hearts are very heavy but a word of encouragement does wonders.

The good man asks advice from friends; the wicked plunges ahead—and fall.

A lazy man won't even dress the game he gets while hunting, but the diligent man makes good use of everything he finds.

The path of the godly leads to life. So why fear Death?

Psalms for the Thirteenth Day

61 O God, listen to me! Hear my prayer!

² For wherever I am, though far away at the ends of the earth, I will cry to You for help. When my heart is faint and overwhelmed, lead me to the mighty, towering Rock of safety. ³ For You are my refuge, a high tower where my enemies can never reach me. ⁴ I shall live forever in Your tabernacle; oh, to be safe beneath the shelter of Your wings. ⁵ For You have heard my vows, O God, to praise You every day, and You have given me the blessings You reserve for those who reverence Your name.

⁶ You will give me added years of life, as rich and full as those of many generations, all packed into one! ⁷ And I shall live before the Lord forever. Oh, send Your lovingkindness and truth to guard and watch over me, ⁸ And I will praise Your name continually, fulfilling my vow of praising You each day.

62 I stand silently before the Lord, waiting for Him to rescue me. For salvation comes from Him alone. ² Yes, He alone is my Rock, my rescuer, defense and fortress. Why then should I be tense with fear when troubles come?

³, ⁴ But what is this? They pick on me at a time when my throne is tottering; they plot my death and

use lies and deceit to try to force me from the throne. They are so friendly to my face while cursing in their hearts! ⁵ But I stand silently before the Lord, waiting for Him to rescue me. For salvation comes from Him alone. ⁶ Yes, He alone is my Rock, my rescuer, defense and fortress — why then should I be tense with fear when troubles come?

⁷ My protection and success come from God alone. He is my refuge, a Rock where no enemy can reach me. ⁸ O my people, trust Him all the time. Pour out your longings before Him, for He can help! ⁹ The greatest of men, or the lowest — both alike are nothing in His sight. They weigh less than air on scales!

¹⁰, ¹¹ Don't become rich by extortion and robbery. And don't let the rich men be proud. ¹² He is loving and kind and rewards each one of us according to the work we do for Him.

(A Psalm of David when he was hiding in the wilderness of Judea.)

63   O God, *my* God! How I search for You! How I thirst for You in this parched and weary land where there is no water! How I long to find You! ² How I wish I could go into Your sanctuary to see Your strength and glory! ³ For Your love and kindness are better to me than life itself. How I praise You! ⁴ I will bless You as long as I live, lifting up my hands to You in prayer. ⁵ At last I shall be fully satisfied; I will praise You with great joy!

⁶ I lie awake at night thinking of You — ⁷ Of how much You have helped me — and how I rejoice through the night beneath the protecting shadow of Your wings. ⁸ I follow close behind You, protected

by Your strong right arm. ⁹ But those plotting to
destroy me shall go down to the depths of hell.
¹⁰ They are doomed to die by the sword, to become
the food of jackals. ¹¹ But I will rejoice in God! All
who trust in Him exult, while liars shall be silenced.

64 Lord, listen to my complaint: Oh, preserve my
life from the conspiracy of these wicked men, these
gangs of criminals. ³ They cut me down with sharp-
ened tongues; they aim their bitter words like arrows
straight at my heart. ⁴ They shoot from ambush at
the innocent. Suddenly the deed is done, yet they are
not afraid. ⁵ They encourage each other do to evil.
They meet in secret to set their traps. "He will never
notice them here," they say. ⁶ They keep a sharp
lookout for opportunities of crime. They spend long
hours with all their endless evil thoughts and plans.

⁷ But God Himself will shoot them down. Suddenly His arrow will pierce them. ⁸ They will stagger
backward, destroyed by those they spoke against. All
who see it happening will scoff at them. ⁹ Then everyone shall stand in awe and confess the greatness of the
miracles of God; at last they will realize what amazing things He does! ¹⁰ And the godly shall rejoice in
the Lord, and trust and praise Him.

65 O God in Zion, we wait before You in silent
praise, and thus fulfill our vow. And because You
answer prayer, all mankind will come to You with
their requests. ³ Though sins fill our hearts, You forgive them all. ⁴ How greatly to be envied are those
You have chosen to come and live with You within the
holy tabernacle courts! What joys await us among all
the good things there. ⁵ With dread deeds and awesome power You will defend us from our enemies, O

God who saves us. You are the only hope of all mankind throughout the world and far away upon the sea.

⁶ He formed the mountains by His mighty strength.
⁷ He quiets the raging oceans and all the world's
clamor. ⁸ In the farthest corners of the earth the
glorious acts of God shall startle everyone. The dawn
and sunset shout for joy! ⁹ He waters the earth to
make it fertile. The rivers of God will not run dry! He
prepares the earth for His people and sends them rich
harvests of grain. ¹⁰ He waters the furrows with
abundant rain. Showers soften the earth, melting the
clods and causing seeds to sprout across the land.
¹¹, ¹² Then He crowns it all with green, lush pastures
in the wilderness; hillsides blossom with joy. ¹³ The
pastures are filled with flocks of sheep, and the valleys
are carpeted with grain. All the world shouts with
joy, and sings.

Proverbs for the Thirteenth Day

13 A wise youth accepts his father's rebuke; a young mocker doesn't.

†

² The good man wins his case by careful argument; the evil-minded only wants to fight.

†

³ Self-control means controlling the tongue! A quick retort can ruin everything.

†

⁴ Lazy people want much but get little, while the diligent are prospering.

†

⁵ A good man hates lies; wicked men lie constantly and come to shame.

†

⁶ A man's goodness helps him all through life, while evil men are being destroyed by their wickedness.

†

⁷ Some rich people are poor, and some poor people have great wealth!

†

⁸ Being kidnaped and held for ransom never worries the poor man!

⁹ The good man's life is full of light. The sinner's road is dark and gloomy.

†

¹⁰ Pride leads to arguments; be humble, take advice and become wise.

†

¹¹ Wealth from gambling quickly disappears; wealth from hard work grows.

†

¹² Hope deferred makes the heart sick; but when dreams come true at last, there is life and joy.

†

¹³ Despise God's Word and find yourself in trouble. Obey it and succeed.

†

¹⁴ The advice of a wise man refreshes like water from a mountain spring. Those accepting it become aware of the pitfalls on ahead.

†

¹⁵ A man with good sense is appreciated. A treacherous man must walk a rocky road.

†

¹⁶ A wise man thinks ahead; a fool doesn't, and even brags about it!

†

¹⁷ An unreliable messenger can cause a lot of trouble. Reliable communication permits progress.

†

¹⁸ If you refuse criticism you will end in poverty and disgrace; if you accept criticism you are on the road to fame.

†

¹⁹ It is pleasant to see plans develop. That is why fools refuse to give them up even when they are wrong.

²⁰ Be with wise men and become wise. Be with evil men and become evil.

†

²¹ Curses chase sinners, while blessings chase the righteous!

†

²² When a good man dies, he leaves an inheritance to his grandchildren; but when a sinner dies, his wealth is stored up for the godly.

†

²³ A poor man's farm may have good soil, but injustice robs him of its riches.

†

²⁴ If you refuse to discipline your son, it proves you don't love him; for if you love him you will be prompt to punish him.

†

²⁵ The good man eats to live, while the evil man lives to eat.

Psalms for the Fourteenth Day

66 Sing to the Lord, all the earth! ² Sing of His glorious name! Tell the world how wonderful He is.

³ How awe-inspiring are Your deeds, O God! How great Your power! No wonder Your enemies surrender! ⁴ All the earth shall worship You and sing of Your glories. ⁵ Come, see the glorious things God has done. What marvelous miracles happen to His people! ⁶ He made a dry road through the sea for them. They went across on foot. What excitement and joy there was that day!

⁷ Because of His great power He rules forever. He watches every movement of the nations. O rebel lands, He will deflate your pride.

⁸ Let everyone bless God and sing His praises, ⁹ For He holds our lives in His hands! And He holds our feet to the path! ¹⁰ You have purified us with fire, O Lord, like silver in a crucible. ¹¹ You captured us in Your net and laid great burdens on our backs. ¹² You sent troops to ride across our broken bodies. We went through fire and flood. But in the end, You brought us into wealth and great abundance.

¹³ Now I have come to Your Temple with burnt-offerings to pay my vows. ¹⁴ For when I was in

trouble I promised You many offerings. [15] That is why I am bringing You these fat he-goats, rams and calves. The smoke of their sacrifice shall rise before You.

[16] Come and hear, all of you who reverence the Lord, and I will tell you what He did for me: [17] For I cried to Him for help, with praises ready on my tongue. [18] He would not have listened if I had not confessed my sins. [19] But He listened! He heard my prayer! He paid attention to it!

[20] Blessed be God who didn't turn away when I was praying, and didn't refuse me His kindness and love.

67 O God, in mercy bless us; let Your face beam with joy as You look down at us.

[2] Send us around the world with the news of Your saving power and Your eternal plan for all mankind. [3] How everyone throughout the earth will praise the Lord! [4] How glad the nations will be, singing for joy because You are their King and will give true justice to their people! [5] Praise God, O world! May all the peoples of the earth give thanks to You. [6, 7] For the earth has yielded abundant harvests. God, even our own God, will bless us. And peoples from remotest lands will worship Him.

68 Arise, O God, and scatter all Your enemies! Chase them away! [2] Drive them off like smoke before the wind; melt them like wax in fire! So let the wicked perish at the presence of God.

[3] But may the godly man exult! May he rejoice and be merry! [4] Sing praises to the Lord! Raise your voice in song to Him who rides upon the clouds!

Jehovah is His name – Oh, rejoice in His presence.
⁵ He is a father to the fatherless; He gives justice to
the widows; for He is holy. ⁶ He gives families to the
lonely, and releases prisoners from jail, singing with
joy! But for rebels there is famine and distress.

⁷ O God, when You led Your people through the
wilderness, ⁸ The earth trembled and the heavens
shook. Mount Sinai quailed before You – the God of
Israel. ⁹, ¹⁰ You sent abundant rain upon Your land,
O God, to refresh it in its weariness! There Your
people lived, for You gave them this home when they
were destitute.

¹¹, ¹², ¹³ The Lord speaks. The enemy flees. The
women at home cry out the happy news: "The armies
that came to destroy us have fled!" Now all the
women of Israel are dividing the booty. See them
sparkle with jewels of silver and gold, covered all over
as wings cover doves! ¹⁴ God scattered their enemies
like snowflakes melting in the forests of Zalmon.

¹⁵, ¹⁶ O mighty mountains in Bashan! O splendid
many-peaked ranges! Well may you look with envy at
Mount Zion, the mount where God has chosen to live
forever. ¹⁷ Surrounded by unnumbered chariots, the
Lord moves on from Mount Sinai and comes to His
holy temple high upon Mount Zion. ¹⁸ He ascends
the heights, leading many captives in His train. He
receives gifts for men, even those who once were
rebels. God will live among us here.

¹⁹ What a glorious Lord! He who daily bears our
burdens also gives us our salvation!

²⁰ He frees us! He rescues us from death. ²¹ But
He will crush His enemies, for they refuse to leave

their guilty, stubborn ways. ²² The Lord says, "Come," to all His people's enemies; they are hiding on Mount Hermon's highest slopes and deep within the sea! ²³ His people must destroy them. Cover your feet with their blood; dogs will eat them.

²⁴ The procession of God my King moves onward to the sanctuary — ²⁵ Singers in front, musicians behind, girls playing the timbrels in between. ²⁶ Let all the people of Israel praise the Lord, who is Israel's fountain. ²⁷ The little tribe of Benjamin leads the way. The princes and elders of Judah, and the princes of Zebulon and Naphtali are right behind. ²⁸ Summon Your might; display Your strength, O God, for You have done such mighty things for us.

²⁹ The kings of the earth are bringing their gifts to Your temple in Jerusalem. ³⁰ Rebuke our enemies, O Lord. Bring them — submissive, tax in hand. Scatter all who delight in war. ³¹ Egypt will send gifts of precious metals. Ethiopia will stretch out her hands to God in adoration. ³² Sing to the Lord, O kingdoms of the earth — sing praises to the Lord, ³³ To Him who rides upon the ancient heavens, whose mighty voice thunders from the sky.

³⁴ Power belongs to God! His majesty shines down on Israel; His strength is mighty in the heavens. ³⁵ What awe we feel, kneeling here before Him in the sanctuary. The God of Israel gives strength and mighty power to His people. Blessed be God!

69 Save me, O my God. The floods have risen. Deeper and deeper I sink in the mire; the waters rise around me. ³ I have wept until I am exhausted; my throat is dry and hoarse; my eyes are swollen with weeping, waiting for my God to act. ⁴ I cannot even count all those who hate me without cause. They are influential men, these who plot to kill me though I am innocent. They demand that I be punished for what I didn't do.

⁵ O God, You know so well how stupid I am, and You know all my sins. ⁶ O Lord God of the armies of heaven, don't let me be a stumbling block to those who trust in You. O God of Israel, don't let me cause them to be confused, ⁷ Though I am mocked and cursed and shamed for Your sake. ⁸ Even my own brothers pretend they don't know me! ⁹ My zeal for God and His work burns hot within me. And because I advocate Your cause, Your enemies insult me even as they insult You. ¹⁰ How they scoff and mock me when I mourn and fast before the Lord! ¹¹ How they talk about me when I wear sackcloth to show my humiliation and sorrow for my sins! ¹² I am the talk of the town and the song of the drunkards. ¹³ But I keep right on praying to you, Lord. For now is the time — You are bending down to hear! You are ready with a plentiful supply of love and kindness! Now answer my prayer and rescue me as You promised. ¹⁴ Pull me out of this mire. Don't let me sink in. Rescue me from those who hate me, and from these deep waters I am in.

¹⁵ Don't let the floods overwhelm me, or the ocean swallow me; save me from the pit that threatens me. ¹⁶ O Jehovah, answer my prayers, for Your loving kindness is wonderful; Your mercy is so plentiful, so tender and so kind. ¹⁷ Don't hide from me; for I am in deep trouble. Quick! Come and save me. ¹⁸ Come, Lord, and rescue me. Ransom me from all my enemies.

¹⁹ You know how they talk about me, and how they so shamefully dishonor me. You see them all and know what each has said.

²⁰ Their contempt has broken my heart; my spirit is heavy within me. If even one would show some pity, if even one would comfort me! ²¹ For food they gave me poison; for my awful thirst they offered me vinegar. ²² Let their joys turn to ashes and their peace disappear; ²³ Let darkness, blindness and great feebleness be theirs. ²⁴ Pour out Your fury upon them; consume them with the fierceness of Your anger. ²⁵ Let their homes be desolate and abandoned. ²⁶ For they persecute the one You have smitten; and scoff at the pain of the one You have pierced. ²⁷ Pile their sins high and do not overlook them. ²⁸ Let these men be blotted from the list of the living; do not give them the joys of life with the righteous.

²⁹ But rescue me, O God, from my poverty and pain. ³⁰ Then I will praise God with my singing! My thanks will be His praise — ³¹ That will please Him more than sacrificing a bullock or an ox. ³² The humble shall see their God at work for them. No wonder they will be so glad! All who seek for God shall live in joy. ³³ For Jehovah hears the cries of His needy ones, and does not look the other way.

³⁴ Praise Him, all heaven and earth! Praise Him, all the seas and everything in them! ³⁵ For God will save Jerusalem; He rebuilds the cities of Judah. His people shall live in them and not be dispossessed. ³⁶ Their children shall inherit the land; all who love His name shall live there safely.

70   Rescue me, O God! Lord, hurry to my aid!

[2, 3] They are after my life, and delight in hurting me. Confuse them! Shame them! Stop them! Don't let them keep on mocking me! [4] But fill the followers of God with joy! Let those who love Your salvation exclaim, "What a wonderful God He is!" [5] But I am in deep trouble. Rush to my aid, for only You can help and save me. O Lord, don't delay.

Proverbs for the Fourteenth Day

14 A wise woman builds her house, while a foolish woman tears hers down by her own efforts.

†

² To do right honors God; to sin is to despise Him.

†

³ A rebel's foolish talk should prick his own pride! But the wise man's speech is respected.

†

⁴ An empty stable stays clean — but there is no income from an empty stable.

†

⁵ A truthful witness never lies; a false witness always lies.

†

⁶ A mocker never finds the wisdom he claims he is looking for, yet it comes easily to the man with common sense.

†

⁷ If you are looking for advice, stay away from fools.

†

⁸ The wise man looks ahead. The fool attempts to fool himself and won't face facts.

†

⁹ The common bond of rebels is their guilt. The common bond of godly people is good will.

¹⁰ Only the person involved can know his own bitterness or joy — no one else can really share it.

†

¹¹ The work of the wicked will perish; the work of the godly will flourish.

†

¹² Before every man there lies a wide and pleasant road that seems right but ends in death.

†

¹³ Laughter cannot mask a heavy heart. When the laughter ends, the grief remains.

†

¹⁴ The backslider gets bored with himself; the godly man's life is exciting.

†

¹⁵ Only a simpleton believes what he is told! A prudent man checks to see where he is going.

†

¹⁶ A wise man is cautious and avoids danger; a fool plunges ahead with great confidence.

†

¹⁷ A short-tempered man is a fool. He hates the man who is patient.

†

¹⁸ The simpleton is crowned with folly; the wise man is crowned with knowledge.

†

¹⁹ Evil men bow before the godly.

†

²⁰ Even his own neighbors despise the poor man, while the rich have many "friends."

†

²¹ To despise the poor is to sin. Blessed are those who pity them.

²² Those who plot evil shall wander away and be lost, but those who plan good shall be granted mercy and quietness.

†

²³ Work brings profit; talk brings poverty!

†

²⁴ Wise men are praised for their wisdom; fools are despised for their folly.

†

²⁵ A witness who tells the truth saves good men from being sentenced to death, but a false witness is a traitor.

†

²⁶ Reverence for God gives a man deep strength; his children have a place of refuge and security.

†

²⁷ Reverence for the Lord is a fountain of life; its waters keep a man from death.

†

²⁸ A growing population is a king's glory; a dwindling nation is his doom.

†

²⁹ A wise man controls his temper. He knows that anger causes mistakes.

†

³⁰ A relaxed attitude lengthens a man's life; jealousy rots it away.

†

³¹ Anyone who oppresses the poor is insulting God who made them. To help the poor is to honor God.

†

³² The godly have a refuge when they die, but the wicked are crushed by their sins.

†

³³ Wisdom is enshrined in the hearts of men of

common sense, but it must shout loudly before fools will hear it.

†

³⁴ Godliness exalts a nation, but sin is a reproach to any people.

†

³⁵ A king rejoices in servants who know what they are doing; he is angry with those who cause trouble.

Psalms for the Fifteenth Day

71 Lord, You are my refuge! Don't let me down!
² Save me from my enemies, for You are just! Rescue
me! Bend down Your ear and listen to my plea and
save me. ³ Be to me a great protecting rock, where I
am always welcome, safe from all attacks. For You
have issued the order to save me. ⁴ Rescue me, O
God, from these unjust and cruel men. ⁵ O Lord, You
alone are my hope; I've trusted You from childhood.
⁶ Yes, You have been with me from birth and have
helped me constantly — no wonder I am always praising You! ⁷ My success — at which so many stand
amazed — is because You are my mighty protector.
⁸ All day long I'll praise and honor You, O God, for
all that You have done for me.

⁹ And now, in my old age, don't set me aside! Don't
forsake me now when my strength is failing! ¹⁰ My
enemies are whispering, ¹¹ "God has forsaken him!
Now we can get him. There is no one to help him
now!" ¹² O God, don't stay away! Come quickly!
Help! ¹³ Destroy them! Cover them with failure and
disgrace — these enemies of mine. ¹⁴ I will keep on
expecting You to help me. I praise You more and
more. ¹⁵ I cannot count the times when You have
faithfully rescued me from danger. I will tell everyone
how good You are, and of Your constant, daily care.

[16] I walk in the strength of the Lord God. I tell everyone that You alone are just and good. [17] O God, You have helped me from my earliest childhood — and I have constantly testified to others of the wonderful things You do. [18] And now that I am old and gray, don't forsake me. Give me time to tell this new generation (and their children too) about all Your mighty miracles. [19] Your power and goodness, Lord, reach to the highest heavens. You have done such wonderful things. Where is there another God like You? [20] You have let me sink down deep in desperate problems. But You will bring me back to life again, up from the depths of the earth. [21] You will give me greater honor than before, and turn again and comfort me.

[22] I will praise You with music, telling of Your faithfulness to all Your promises, O Holy One of Israel. [23] I will shout and sing Your praises for redeeming me. [24] I will talk to others all day long about Your justice and Your goodness. For all who tried to hurt me have been disgraced and dishonored.

72 O God, help the king to judge as You would, and help his son to walk in godliness. [2] Help him to give justice to Your people, even to the poor! [3] May the mountains and hills flourish in prosperity because of his good reign. [4] Help him to defend the poor and needy and to crush their oppressors. [5] May the poor and needy revere You constantly, as long as sun and moon continue in the skies! Yes, forever!

[6] May the reign of this Son of mine be as gentle and fruitful as the springtime rains upon the grass — like showers that water the earth! [7] May all good men flourish in His reign, with abundance of peace to the end of time. [8] Let Him reign from sea to sea, and

from the Euphrates River to the ends of the earth. [9] The desert nomads shall bow before Him! His enemies shall fall face downward in the dust. [10] Kings along the Mediterranean coast — the kings of Tarshish and the islands — and those from Sheba and from Seba — all will bring their gifts. [11] Yes, kings from everywhere! All will bow before Him! All will serve Him!

[12] He will take care of the helpless and poor when they cry to Him; for they have no one else to defend them. [13] He feels pity for the weak and needy, and will rescue them. [14] He will save them from oppression and from violence, for their lives are precious to Him.

[15] And He shall live; and to Him will be given the gold of Sheba, and there will be constant praise for Him. His people will bless Him all day long. [16] Bless us with abundant crops throughout the land, even on the highland plains; may there be fruit like that of Lebanon; may the cities be as full of people as the fields are of grass. [17] His name will be honored forever; it will continue as the sun; and all will be blessed in Him; all nations will praise Him.

[18] Blessed be Jehovah God, the God of Israel, who only does wonderful things! [19] Blessed be His glorious name forever! Let the whole earth be filled with His glory. Amen, and amen!

[20] (This ends the psalms of David, son of Jesse.)

73 How good God is to Israel — to those whose hearts are pure. [2] But as for me, I came *so* close to the edge of the cliff! My feet were slipping and I was almost gone. [3] For I was envious of the prosperity of the proud and wicked. [4] Yes, all through life their road is smooth! They grow sleek and fat. [5] They aren't always in trouble and plagued with problems like everyone else, [6] So their pride sparkles like a jeweled necklace, and their clothing is woven of cruelty! [7] These fat cats have everything their hearts could ever wish for! [8] They scoff at God and threaten His people. How proudly they speak! [9] They boast against the very heavens, and their words strut through the earth.

[10] And so God's people are dismayed and confused, and drink it all in. [11] "Does God realize what is going on?" they ask. [12] "Look at these men of arrogance; they never have to lift a finger — theirs is a life of ease; and all the time their riches multiply." [13] Have I been wasting my time? Why take the trouble to be pure? [14] All I get out of it is trouble and woe — every day and all day long! [15] If I had really said that, I would have been a traitor to Your people. [16] Yet it is so hard to explain it — this prosperity of those who hate the Lord. [17] Then one day I went into God's sanctuary to meditate, and thought about the future of these evil men. [18] What a slippery path they are on — suddenly God will send them sliding over the edge of the cliff and down to their destruction: [19] An instant end to all their happiness, an eternity of terror. [20] Their present life is only a dream! They will awaken to the truth as one awakens from a dream of things that never really were!

[21] When I saw this, what turmoil filled my heart! [22] I saw myself so stupid and so ignorant; I must seem like an animal to You, O God. [23] But even so, You love me! You are holding my right hand! [24] You will keep on guiding me all my life with Your wisdom and

counsel; and afterwards receive me into the glories of heaven! [25] Whom have I in heaven but You? And I desire no one on earth as much as You! [26] My health fails; my spirits droop, yet God remains! He is the strength of my heart; He is mine forever!

[27] But those refusing to worship God will perish, for He destroys those serving other gods.

[28] But as for me, I get as close to Him as I can! I have chosen Him and I will tell everyone about the wonderful ways He rescues me.

74 O God, why have You cast us away forever? Why is Your anger hot against us — the sheep of Your own pasture? [2] Remember that we are Your people — the ones You chose in ancient times from slavery and made the choicest of Your possessions. You chose Jerusalem as Your home on earth!

[3] Walk through the awful ruins of the city, and see what the enemy has done to Your sanctuary. [4] There they shouted their battle cry and erected their idols to flaunt their victory. [5, 6] Everything lies in shambles like a forest chopped to the ground. They came with their axes and sledgehammers and smashed and chopped the carved paneling, [7] And set the sanctuary on fire, and razed it to the ground — Your sanctuary, Lord. [8] "Let's wipe out every trace of God," they said, and went through the entire country burning down the assembly places where we worshiped You.

[9, 10] There is nothing left to show that we are Your people. The prophets are gone, and who can say when it all will end? How long, O God, will You allow our enemies to dishonor Your name? Will You let them

get away with this forever? [11] Why do You delay? Why hold back Your power? Unleash Your fist and give them a final blow.

[12] God is my King from ages past; You have been actively helping me everywhere throughout the land. [13, 14] You divided the Red Sea with Your strength; You crushed the sea-god's heads! You gave him to the desert tribes to eat! [15] At Your command the springs burst forth to give Your people water; and then You dried a path for them across the everflowing Jordan. [16] Day and night alike belong to You; You made the starlight and the sun. [17] All nature is within Your hands; You make the summer and the winter too. [18] Lord, see how these enemies scoff at You. O Jehovah, an arrogant nation has blasphemed Your name.

[19] O Lord, save me! Protect Your turtle-dove from the hawks. Save Your beloved people from these beasts. [20] Remember Your promise! For the land is full of darkness and cruel men. [21] O Lord, don't let Your downtrodden people be constantly insulted. Give cause for these poor and needy ones to praise Your name! [22] Arise, O God, and state Your case against our enemies. Remember the insults these rebels have hurled against You all day long. [23] Don't overlook the cursing of these enemies of Yours; it grows louder and louder.

75 How we thank You, Lord! Your mighty miracles give proof that You care.

[2] "Yes," the Lord replies, "And when I am ready, I will punish the wicked! [3] Though the earth shakes and all its people live in turmoil, yet its pillars are firm, for I have set them in place!"

[4] I warned the proud to cease their arrogance! I

told the wicked to lower their insolent gaze, ⁵ And to stop being stubborn and proud. ^{6, 7} For promotion and power come from nowhere on earth, but only from God. He promotes one and deposes another. ⁸ In Jehovah's hand there is a cup of pale and sparkling wine. It is His judgment, poured out upon the wicked of the earth. They must drain that cup to the dregs. ⁹ But as for me, I shall forever declare the praises of the God of Jacob. ¹⁰ "I will cut off the strength of evil men," says the Lord, "and increase the power of good men in their place."

Proverbs for the Fifteenth Day

15 A soft answer turns away wrath, but harsh words cause quarrels.

†

² A wise teacher makes learning a joy; a rebellious teacher spouts foolishness.

†

³ The Lord is watching everywhere and keeps His eye on both the evil and the good.

†

⁴ Gentle words cause life and health; griping brings discouragement.

†

⁵ Only a fool despises his father's advice; a wise son considers each suggestion.

†

⁶ There is treasure in being good, but trouble dogs the wicked.

†

⁷ Only the good can give good advice. Rebels can't.

†

⁸ The Lord hates the gifts of the wicked, but delights in the prayers of His people.

†

⁹, ¹⁰ The Lord despises the deeds of the wicked, but loves those who try to be good. If they stop trying,

the Lord will punish them; if they rebel against that punishment, they will die.

†

¹¹ The depths of hell are open to God's knowledge. How much more the hearts of all mankind!

†

¹² A mocker stays away from wise men because he hates to be scolded.

†

¹³ A happy face means a glad heart; a sad face means a breaking heart.

†

¹⁴ A wise man is hungry for truth, while the mocker feeds on trash.

†

¹⁵ When a man is gloomy, everything seems to go wrong; when he is cheerful, everything seems right!

†

¹⁶ Better a little with reverence for God, than great treasure and trouble with it.

†

¹⁷ It is better to eat soup with someone you love than steak with someone you hate.

†

¹⁸ A quick-tempered man starts fights; a cool-tempered man tries to stop them.

†

¹⁹ A lazy fellow has trouble all through life; the good man's path is easy!

†

²⁰ A sensible son gladdens his father. A rebellious son saddens his mother.

†

²¹ If a man enjoys folly, something is wrong! The sensible stay on the pathways of right.

²² Plans go wrong with too few counselors; many counselors bring success.

†

²³ Everyone enjoys giving good advice, and how wonderful it is to be able to say the right thing at the right time!

†

²⁴ The road of the godly leads upward, leaving hell behind.

†

²⁵ The Lord destroys the possessions of the proud but cares for widows.

†

²⁶ The Lord hates the thoughts of the wicked but delights in kind words.

†

²⁷ Dishonest money brings grief to all the family, but hating bribes brings happiness.

†

²⁸ A good man thinks before he speaks; the evil man pours out his evil words without a thought.

†

²⁹ The Lord is far from the wicked, but He hears the prayers of the righteous.

†

³⁰ Pleasant sights and good reports give happiness and health.

†

^{31, 32} If you profit from constructive criticism you will be elected to the wise men's hall of fame. But to reject criticism is to harm yourself and your own best interests.

†

³³ Humility and reverence for the Lord will make you both wise and honored.

Psalms for the Sixteenth Day

76 God's reputation is very great in Judah and in Israel! [2] His home is in Jerusalem! He lives upon Mount Zion. [3] There He breaks the weapons of our enemies.

[4] The everlasting mountains cannot compare with You in glory! [5] The mightiest of our enemies are conquered; they lie before us in the sleep of death; not one can lift a hand against us. [6] When You rebuked them, God of Jacob, steeds and riders fell. [7] No wonder You are greatly feared! Who can stand before an angry God? [8] You pronounce sentence on them from heaven; the earth trembles and stands silently before You; [9] You stand up to punish the evil-doers and to defend the meek of the earth.

[10] Man's futile wrath will bring You glory! You will use it as an ornament! [11] Fulfill all your vows that you have made to Jehovah your God. Let everyone bring Him presents. He should be reverenced and feared, [12] For He cuts down princes and does awesome things to the kings of the earth.

77 I cry to the Lord; I call and call to Him. Oh, that He would listen. [2] I am in deep trouble and I need His help so badly. All night long I pray, lifting my hands to heaven, pleading. There can be no joy for me until He acts. ³ I think of God and moan, over-whelmed with longing for His help. ⁴ I cannot sleep until You act. I am too distressed even to pray!

⁵ I keep thinking of the good old days of the past, long since ended. ⁶ Then my nights were filled with joyous songs. I search my soul and meditate upon the difference now. ⁷ Has the Lord rejected me forever? Will He never again be favorable? ⁸ Is His loving-kindness gone forever? Has His promise failed? ⁹ Has He forgotten to be kind to one so undeserving? Has He slammed the door in anger on His love? ¹⁰ And I said: This is my fate, that the blessings of God have changed to hate. ¹¹ I recall the many miracles He did for me so long ago. ¹² Those wonderful deeds are constantly in my thoughts. I cannot stop thinking about them. ¹³ O God, Your ways are holy. Where is there any other as mighty as You? ¹⁴ You are the God of miracles and wonders! You still demonstrate Your awesome power.

¹⁵ You have redeemed us who are the sons of Jacob and of Joseph by Your might. ¹⁶ When the Red Sea saw You, how it feared! It trembled to its depths! ¹⁷ The clouds poured down their rain, the thunder rolled and crackled in the sky. Your lightning flashed. ¹⁸ There was thunder in the whirlwind; the lightning lighted up the world! The earth trembled and shook. ¹⁹ Your road led by a pathway through the sea — a pathway no one knew was there! ²⁰ You led Your people along that road like a flock of sheep, with Moses and Aaron as their shepherds.

78 O my people, listen to my teaching. Open your ears to what I am saying. ², ³ For I will show you lessons from our history, stories handed down to us from former generations. ⁴ I will reveal these truths to you so that you can describe these glorious deeds of Jehovah to your children, and tell them about the mighty miracles He did. ⁵ For He gave His laws to Israel, and commanded our fathers to teach them to their children, ⁶ So that they in turn could teach their children too. Thus His laws pass down from generation to generation. ⁷ In this way each generation has been able to obey His laws and to set its hope anew on God and not forget His glorious miracles. ⁸ Thus they did not need to be as their fathers were — stubborn, rebellious, unfaithful, refusing to give their hearts to God.

⁹ The people of Ephraim, though fully armed, were defeated in battle ¹⁰ Because they didn't obey His laws. They refused to follow His ways. ¹¹, ¹² And they forgot about the wonderful miracles God had done for them, and for their fathers back in Egypt. ¹³ For He divided the sea before them and led them through! The water stood banked up along both sides of them! ¹⁴ In the daytime He led them by a cloud, and at night by a pillar of fire. ¹⁵ He split open the rocks in the wilderness to give them plenty of water, as though gushing from a spring. ¹⁶ Streams poured from the rock, flowing like a river! ¹⁷ Yet they kept on with their rebellion, sinning against the God who is above all gods. ¹⁸ They murmured and complained, demanding other food than God was giving them. ¹⁹, ²⁰ They even spoke against God Himself. "Why can't He give us decent food as well as water?" they grumbled. ²¹ Jehovah heard them and was angry; the fire of His wrath burned against Israel, ²² Because they didn't believe in God or trust in Him to care for them, ²³ Even though He commanded the

skies to open — He opened the windows of heaven — ²⁴ And rained down manna for their food. He gave them bread from heaven! ²⁵ They ate angels' food! He gave them all that they could hold.

²⁶ And He led forth the east wind and guided the south wind by His mighty power. ²⁷ He rained down birds as thick as dust, clouds of them like sands along the shore! ²⁸ He caused the birds to fall near the ground among the tents! ²⁹ The people ate their fill. He gave them what they asked for. ³⁰ But they had hardly finished eating, and the meat was yet in their mouths, ³¹ When the anger of the Lord rose against them and killed the finest of Israel's young men. ³² Yet even so the people kept on sinning and refused to believe in miracles. ³³ So He cut their lives short and gave them years of terror and disaster.

³⁴ Then at last, when He had ruined them, they walked awhile behind Him; how earnestly they turned around and followed Him! ³⁵ Then they remembered that God was their Rock — that their Savior was the God above all gods. ³⁶ But it was only with their words they followed Him, not with their hearts; ³⁷ Their hearts were far away. They did not keep their promises. ³⁸ Yet He was merciful and forgave their sins and didn't destroy them all. Many and many a time He held back His anger. ³⁹ For He remembered that they were merely mortal men, gone in a moment like a breath of wind.

⁴⁰ Oh, how often they rebelled against Him in those desert years and grieved His heart. ⁴¹ Again and again they turned away and tempted God to kill them, and limited the Holy One of Israel from giving them His blessings. ⁴² They forgot His power and love,

and how He had rescued them from their enemies; [43] They forgot the plagues He sent upon the Egyptians in Tanis — [44] How He turned their rivers into blood, so that no one could drink; [45] And how He sent vast swarms of flies to fill the land, and how the frogs had covered all of Egypt!

[46] He gave their crops to caterpillars. Their harvest was consumed by locusts. [47] He destroyed their grapevines and their sycamores with hail. [48] Their cattle died in the fields, mortally wounded by iceballs from heaven. Their sheep were killed by lightning. [49] He loosed on them the fierceness of His anger, sending sorrow and trouble. He dispatched against them a band of destroying angels. [50] He gave free course to His anger and did not spare the Egyptians' lives, but handed them over to plagues and sickness. [51] Then He killed the eldest son in each Egyptian family — he who was the beginning of its strength and joy.

[52] But He led forth His own people like a flock, guiding them safely through the wilderness. [53] He kept them safe, so they were not afraid. But the Sea closed in upon their enemies and overwhelmed them. [54] He brought them to the border of His land of blessing, to this land of hills He made for them. [55] He drove out the nations occupying the land, and gave each tribe of Israel its apportioned place as its home.

[56] Yet though He did all this for them, they still rebelled against the God above all gods, and refused to follow His commands. [57] They turned back from entering the Promised Land and disobeyed as their fathers had. Like a crooked arrow, they missed the target of God's will. [58] They made Him angry by erecting idols and altars to other gods.

⁵⁹ When God saw their deeds, His wrath was strong and He despised His people. ⁶⁰ Then He abandoned His tabernacle at Shiloh, where He had lived among mankind, ⁶¹ And allowed His ark to be captured; He surrendered His glory into enemy hands. ⁶² He caused His people to be butchered because His anger was intense. ⁶³ Their young men were killed by fire and their girls died before they were old enough to sing their wedding songs. ⁶⁴ The priests were slaughtered and their widows died before they could even begin their lament. ⁶⁵ Then the Lord rose up as though awakening from sleep, and like a mighty man aroused by wine ⁶⁶ He routed His enemies and drove them back and sent them to eternal shame. ⁶⁷ But He rejected Joseph's family, the tribe of Ephraim, ⁶⁸ And chose the tribe of Judah — and Mount Zion which He loved. ⁶⁹ There He built His towering temple, solid and enduring as the heavens and the earth. ⁷⁰ He chose His servant David, taking him from feeding sheep, ⁷¹, ⁷² And from following the ewes with lambs; God presented David to His people as their shepherd and he cared for them with a true heart and skillful hands.

79 O God, Your land has been conquered by the heathen nations. Your Temple is defiled and Jerusalem is a heap of ruins. ² The bodies of Your people lie exposed — food for birds and animals. ³ The enemy has butchered the entire population of Jerusalem; blood has flowed like water; no one is left even to bury them. ⁴ The nations all around us scoff. They heap contempt on us.

⁵ O Jehovah, how long will You be angry with us? Forever? Will Your jealousy burn till every hope is

gone? [6] Pour out Your wrath upon the godless nations, not on us! And on kingdoms that refuse to pray, that will not call upon Your name! [7] For they have destroyed Your people Israel, invading every home. [8] Oh, do not hold us guilty for our former sins! Let Your tenderhearted mercies meet our needs, for we are brought low to the dust. [9] Help us, God of our salvation! Help us for the honor of Your name! Oh, save us and forgive our sins. [10] Why should the heathen nations be allowed to scoff, "Where is their God?" Publicly avenge this slaughter of Your people! [11] Listen to the sighing of the prisoners and those condemned to die. Demonstrate the greatness of Your power by saving them. [12] O Lord, take sevenfold vengeance on these nations scorning You.

[13] Then we Your people, the sheep of Your pasture, will thank You forever and forever, praising Your greatness from generation to generation.

Proverbs for the Sixteenth Day

16 We can make our plans, but the final outcome is in God's hands.

†

² We can always "prove" that we are right, but is the Lord convinced?

†

³ Commit your work to the Lord, then it will succeed.

†

⁴ The Lord has made everything for His own purposes — even the wicked, for punishment.

†

⁵ Pride disgusts the Lord. Take my word for it — *proud men shall be punished*.

†

⁶ Iniquity is atoned for by mercy and truth; being good comes from reverence for God.

†

⁷ When a man is trying to please God, He makes even his worst enemies to be at peace with him.

†

⁸ A little, gained honestly, is better than great wealth gotten by dishonest means.

⁹ We should make plans — counting on God to direct us.

†

¹⁰ God will help the king to judge the people fairly; there need be no mistakes.

†

¹¹ The Lord demands fairness in every business deal. He established this principle.

†

¹² It is a horrible thing for a king to do evil. His right to rule depends upon his fairness.

†

¹³ The king rejoices when his people are truthful and fair.

†

¹⁴ The anger of the king is a messenger of death and a wise man will appease it.

†

¹⁵ Many favors are showered on those who please the king.

†

¹⁶ How much better is wisdom than gold, and understanding than silver!

†

¹⁷ The path of the godly leads away from evil; he who follows that path is safe.

†

¹⁸ Pride goes before destruction and haughtiness before a fall.

†

¹⁹ Better poor and humble than proud and rich.

20 God blesses those who obey Him; happy the man who trusts in the Lord.

†

21 The wise man is known by his common sense, and a pleasant teacher is the best.

†

22 Wisdom is a fountain of life to those possessing it, but a fool's burden is his folly.

†

23 From a wise mind comes careful and persuasive speech.

†

24 Kind words are like honey — enjoyable and healthful.

†

25 Before every man there lies a wide and pleasant road he thinks is right, but it ends in death.

†

26 Hunger is good — if it makes you work to satisfy it!

†

27 Idle hands are the devil's workshop; idle lips are his mouthpiece.

†

28 An evil man sows strife; gossip separates the best of friends.

†

29 Wickedness loves company — and leads others into sin.

†

30 The wicked man stares into space with pursed lips, deep in thought, planning his evil deeds.

³¹ White hair is a crown of glory and is seen most among the godly.

†

³² It is better to be slow-tempered than famous; it is better to have self-control than to control an army.

†

³³ We toss the coin, but it is the Lord who controls its decision.

Psalms for the Seventeenth Day

80 O Shepherd of Israel who leads Israel like a flock; O God enthroned above the cherubim, bend down Your ear and listen as I plead. Display Your power and radiant glory. ² Let Ephraim, Benjamin and Manasseh see You rouse Yourself and use Your mighty power to rescue us.

³ Turn us again to Yourself, O God. Look down on us in joy and love; only then shall we be saved. ⁴ O Jehovah, God of heaven's armies, how long will You be angry and reject our prayers? ⁵ You have fed us with sorrow and tears, ⁶ And have made us the scorn of the neighboring nations. They laugh among themselves.

⁷ Turn us again to Yourself, O God of Hosts. Look down on us in joy and love; only then shall we be saved. ⁸ You brought us from Egypt as though we were a tender vine and drove away the heathen from Your land and planted us. ⁹ You cleared the ground and tilled the soil and we took root and filled the land. ¹⁰ The mountains were covered with our shadow; we were like the mighty cedar trees, ¹¹ Covering the entire land from the Mediterranean Sea to the Euphrates River. ¹² But now You have broken down our walls leaving us without protection. ¹³ The boar from the forest roots around us, and the wild animals feed on us.

¹⁴ Come back, we beg of You, O God of the armies of heaven, and bless us. Look down from heaven and see our plight and care for this Your vine! ¹⁵ Protect what You Yourself have planted, this son You have raised for Yourself. ¹⁶ For we are chopped and burned by our enemies. May they perish at Your frown. ¹⁷ Strengthen the man You love, the son of Your choice, ¹⁸ And we will never forsake You again. Revive us to trust in You.

¹⁹ Turn us again to Yourself, O God of the armies of heaven. Look down on us, Your face aglow with joy and love — only then shall we be saved.

81 The Lord makes us strong! Sing praises! Sing to Israel's God!

² Sing, accompanied by drums; pluck the sweet lyre and harp. ³ Sound the trumpet! Come to the joyous celebrations at full moon, new moon and all the other holidays! ⁴ For God has given us these times of joy; they are scheduled in the laws of Israel. ⁵ He gave them as reminders of His war against Egypt where we were slaves on foreign soil.

I heard an unknown voice that said, ⁶ "Now I will relieve your shoulder of its burden; I will free your hands from their heavy tasks." ⁷ He said, "You cried to Me in trouble and I saved you; I answered from Mount Horeb where the thunder hides. I tested your faith at Meribah, when you complained there was no water. ⁸ Listen to Me, O My people, while I give you stern warnings. O Israel, if you will only listen! ⁹ *You must never worship any other god,* nor ever have an idol in your home. ¹⁰ For it was I, Jehovah your God, who brought you out of the land of Egypt. Only test Me! Open your mouth wide and see if I won't fill it! You will receive every blessing you can use! ¹¹ But no, My people won't listen. Israel doesn't want Me around. ¹² So I am letting them go their blind and stubborn way, living according to their own desires.

¹³ But oh, that My people would listen to Me! Oh, that Israel would follow Me, walking in My paths! ¹⁴ How quickly then I would subdue her enemies! How soon My hands would be upon her foes! ¹⁵ Those who hate the Lord would cringe before Him; their desolation would last forever. ¹⁶ But He would feed you with the choicest foods. He would satisfy you with honey for the taking.

82 God stands up to open heaven's court. He pronounces judgment on the judges. ² How long will you judges refuse to listen to the evidence? How long will you shower special favors on the wicked? ³ Give fair judgment to the poor man, the afflicted, the fatherless, the destitute. ⁴ Rescue the poor and needy from the grasp of evil men. ⁵ But you are so foolish and so ignorant! Because you are in darkness, all the foundations of society are shaken to the core. ⁶ I have called you all "gods" and "sons of the Most High." ⁷ But in death you are mere men. You will fall as any prince — for all must die.

⁸ Stand up, O God, and judge the earth. For all of it belongs to You. All nations are in Your hands.

83 O God, don't sit idly by, silent and inactive when we pray. Answer us! Deliver us!

²Don't You hear the tumult and commotion of Your enemies? Don't You see what they are doing, these proud men who hate the Lord? ³ They are full of craftiness and plot against Your people, laying plans to slay Your precious ones. ⁴ Come, they say, and let us wipe out Israel as a nation — we will de-

stroy the very memory of her existence. ⁵ This was their unanimous decision at their summit conference — they signed a treaty to ally themselves against Almighty God — ⁶ These Ishmaelites and Edomites and Moabites and Hagrites; ⁷ People from the lands of Gebal, Ammon, Amalek, Philistia and Tyre; ⁸ Assyria has joined them too, and is allied with the descendants of Lot.

⁹ Do to them as once You did to Midian, or as You did to Sisera and Jabin at the river Kishon, ¹⁰ And as You did to Your enemies at Endor, whose decaying corpses fertilized the soil. ¹¹ Make their mighty nobles die as Oreb did, and Zeeb; let all their princes die like Zebah and Zalmunna, ¹² Who said, "Let us seize for our own use these pasturelands of God!"

¹³ Oh my God, blow them away like dust; like chaff before the wind — ¹⁴ As a forest fire that roars across a mountain. ¹⁵ Chase them with Your fiery storms, tempests and tornados. ¹⁶ Utterly disgrace them until they recognize Your power and name, O Lord. ¹⁷ Make them failures in everything they do; let them be ashamed and terrified ¹⁸ Until they learn that You alone, Jehovah, are the God above all gods in supreme charge of all the earth.

84 How lovely is Your temple, O Lord of the armies of heaven.

² I long, yes, faint with longing to be able to enter Your courtyard and come near to the Living God. ³ Even the sparrows and swallows are welcome to come and nest among Your altars and there have their young, O Lord of heaven's armies, my King and my God! ⁴ How happy are Your priests who can always be in Your Temple, singing Your praises.

⁵ Happy are those who are strong in the Lord, who want above all else to follow Your steps. ⁶ When they walk through the Valley of Weeping it will become a place of springs where pools of blessing and refreshment collect after rains! ⁷ They will grow constantly in strength and each of them is invited to meet with the Lord in Zion!

⁸ O Jehovah, God of the heavenly armies, hear my prayer! Listen, God of Israel. ⁹ O God, our Defender and our Shield, have mercy on the one You have anointed as Your king.

¹⁰ A single day spent in Your Temple is better than a thousand anywhere else! I would rather be a doorman of the Temple of my God than live in palaces of wickedness. ¹¹ For Jehovah God is our Light and our Protector. He gives us grace and glory. No good thing will He withhold from those who walk along His paths.

¹² O Lord of the armies of heaven, blessed are those who trust in You.

85 Lord, You have poured out amazing blessings on this land! You have restored the fortunes of Israel, ² And forgiven the sins of Your people — yes, covered over each one, ³ So that all Your wrath, Your blazing anger, is now ended.

⁴ Now bring us back to loving You, O Lord, so that Your anger will never need rise against us again. ⁵ (Or will You be always angry — on and on to distant generations?) ⁶ Oh, revive us! Then Your people can rejoice in You again. ⁷ Pour out Your love and kindness on us, Lord, and grant us Your salvation.

⁸ I am listening carefully to all the Lord is saying

— for He speaks peace to His people, His saints, if they will only stop their sinning. ⁹ Surely His salvation is near to those who reverence Him; our land will be filled with His glory!

¹⁰ Mercy and truth have met together. Grim justice and peace have kissed! ¹¹ Truth rises from the earth and righteousness smiles down from heaven.

¹² Yes, the Lord pours down His blessings on the land and it yields its bountiful crops. ¹³ Justice goes before Him to make a pathway for His steps.

Proverbs for the Seventeenth Day

17 A dry crust eaten in peace is better then steak every day along with argument and strife.

†

² A wise slave will rule his master's wicked sons and share their estate.

†

³ Silver and gold are purified by fire, but God purifies hearts.

†

⁴ The wicked enjoy fellowship with others who are wicked; liars enjoy liars.

†

⁵ Mocking the poor is mocking the God who made them. He will punish those who rejoice at others' misfortunes.

†

⁶ An old man's grandchildren are his crowning glory. A child's glory is his father.

†

⁷ Truth from a rebel or lies from a king are both unexpected.

†

⁸ A bribe works like magic. Whoever uses it will prosper!

⁹ Love forgets mistakes; nagging about them parts the best of friends.

†

¹⁰ A rebuke to a man of common sense is more effective than a hundred lashes on the back of a rebel.

†

¹¹ The wicked live for rebellion! they shall be severely punished.

†

¹² It is safer to meet a bear robbed of her cubs than a fool caught in his folly.

†

¹³ If you repay evil for good, a curse is upon your home.

†

¹⁴ It is hard to stop a quarrel once it starts, so don't let it begin.

†

¹⁵ The Lord despises those who say that bad is good, and good is bad.

†

¹⁶ It is senseless to pay tuition to educate a rebel who has no heart for truth.

†

¹⁷ A true friend is always loyal, and a brother is born to help in time of need.

†

¹⁸ It is poor judgment to countersign another's note, to become responsible for his debts.

†

¹⁹ Sinners love to fight; boasting is looking for trouble.

²⁰ An evil man is suspicious of everyone and tumbles into constant trouble.

†

²¹ It's no fun to be a rebel's father.

†

²² A cheerful heart does good like medicine, but a broken spirit makes one sick.

†

²³ It is wrong to accept a bribe to twist justice.

†

²⁴ Wisdom is the main pursuit of sensible men, but a fool's goals are at the ends of the earth!

†

²⁵ A rebellious son is a grief to his father and a bitter blow to his mother.

†

²⁶ How short-sighted to fine the godly for being good! And to punish nobles for being honest!

†

²⁷, ²⁸ The man of few words and settled mind is wise; therefore, even a fool is thought to be wise when he is silent. It pays him to keep his mouth shut.

Psalms for the Eighteenth Day

86 Bend down and hear my prayer, O Lord, and answer me, for I am deep in trouble.

² Protect me from death, for I try to follow all Your laws. Save me, for I am serving You and trusting You. ³ Be merciful, O Lord, for I am looking up to You in constant hope. ⁴ Give me happiness, O Lord, for I worship only You. ⁵ O Lord, You are so good and kind, so ready to forgive; so full of mercy for all who ask Your aid.

⁶ Listen closely to my prayer, O God. Hear my urgent cry. ⁷ I will call to You whenever trouble strikes, and You will help me.

⁸ Where among the heathen gods is there a God like You? Where are their miracles? ⁹ All the nations — and You made each one — will come and bow before You, Lord, and praise Your great and holy name. ¹⁰ For You are great, and do great miracles. You alone are God.

¹¹ Tell me where You want me to go and I will go there. May every fiber of my being unite in reverence to Your name. ¹² With all my heart I will praise You. I will give glory to Your name forever, ¹³ For You love me so much! And You are constantly so kind!

And You have rescued me from deepest hell.

¹⁴ O God, proud and insolent men defy me; violent, godless men are trying to kill me. ¹⁵ But You are merciful and gentle, Lord, slow in getting angry, full of constant lovingkindness and of truth;

¹⁶ So look down in pity and grant strength to Your servant and save me. ¹⁷ Send me a sign of Your favor. When those who hate me see it they will lose face because You help and comfort me.

87 High on His holy mountain stands Jerusalem, the city of God, the city He loves more than any other!

³ O City of God, what wondrous tales are told of you! ⁴ Nowadays when I mention among my friends the names of Egypt and Babylonia, Philistia and Tyre, or even distant Ethiopia, someone boasts that he was born in one or another of those countries.

⁵ But someday the highest honor will be to be a native of Jerusalem! For the God above all gods will personally bless this city. ⁶ When He registers her citizens He will place a checkmark beside the names of those who were born here! ⁷ And in the festivals they'll sing, "All my heart is in Jerusalem."

88 O Jehovah, God of my salvation, I have wept before you day and night. ² Now hear my prayers; oh, listen to my cry,

³ For my life is full of troubles, and death draws near. ⁴ They say my life is ebbing out — a hopeless case. ⁵ They have left me here to die, like those slain on battlefields, from whom Your mercies are removed. ⁶ You have thrust me down to the darkest depths. ⁷ Your wrath lies heavy on me; wave after wave en-

gulfs me. ⁸ You have made my friends to loathe me, and they have gone away. I am in a trap with no way out. ⁹ My eyes grow dim with weeping. Each day I beg Your help; O Lord, I reach my pleading hands to You for mercy.

¹⁰ Soon it will be too late! Of what use are Your miracles when I am in the grave? How can I praise You then? ¹¹ Can those in the grave declare Your lovingkindness? Can they proclaim Your faithfulness? ¹² Can the darkness speak of Your miracles? Can anyone in the Land of Forgetfulness talk about Your help?

¹³ O Lord, I plead for my life and shall keep on pleading day by day. ¹⁴ O Jehovah, why have You thrown my life away? Why are You turning Your face from me, and looking the other way? ¹⁵ From my youth I have been sickly and ready to die. I stand helpless before Your terrors. ¹⁶ Your fierce wrath has overwhelmed me. Your terrors have cut me off. ¹⁷ They flow around me all day long. ¹⁸ Lover, friend, acquaintance — all are gone. There is only darkness everywhere.

89 Forever and ever I will sing about the tender kindness of the Lord! Young and old shall hear about Your blessings. ² Your love and kindness are forever; Your truth is as enduring as the heavens.

³, ⁴ The Lord God says, "I have made a solemn agreement with My chosen servant David. I have taken an oath to establish his descendants as kings forever on his throne, from now until eternity!"

⁵ All heaven shall praise Your miracles, O Lord; myriads of angels will praise You for Your faithful-

ness. [6] For who in all of heaven can be compared with God? What mightiest angel is anything like Him? [7] The highest of angelic powers stand in dread and awe of Him. Who is as revered as He by those surrounding Him? [8] O Jehovah, commander of the heavenly armies, where is there any other Mighty One like You? Faithfulness is Your very character.

[9] You rule the oceans when their waves arise in fearful storms; You speak, and they lie still. [10] You have cut haughty Egypt to pieces. Your enemies are scattered by Your awesome power. [11] The heavens are Yours, the world, everything — for You created them all. [12] You created north and south! Mount Tabor and Mount Hermon rejoice to be signed by Your name as their maker! [13] Strong is Your arm! Strong is Your hand! Your right hand is lifted high in glorious strength.

[14, 15] Your throne is founded on two strong pillars — the one is Justice and the other Righteousness. Mercy and Truth walk before You as Your attendants. Blessed are those who hear the joyful blast of the trumpet, for they shall walk in the light of Your presence. [16] They rejoice all day long in Your wonderful reputation and in Your perfect righteousness. [17] You are their strength! What glory! Our power is based on Your favor! [18] Yes, our protection is from the Lord Himself and He, the Holy One of Israel has given us our king.

[19] In a vision You spoke to Your prophet and said, "I have chosen a splendid young man from the common people to be the king — [20] He is My servant David! I have anointed him with My holy oil. [21] I will steady him and make him strong. [22] His enemies

shall not outwit him, nor shall the wicked overpower him. ²³ I will beat down his adversaries before him, and destroy those who hate him. ²⁴ I will protect and bless him constantly and surround him with my love; he will be great because of Me. ²⁵ He will hold sway from the Euphrates River to the Mediterranean Sea. ²⁶ And he will cry to Me, 'You are my Father, my God, and my Rock of Salvation.'

²⁷ I will treat him as My firstborn son, and make him the mightiest king in all the earth. ²⁸ I will love him forever, and be kind to him always; My covenant with him will never end. ²⁹ He will always have an heir; his throne will be as endless as the days of heaven. ³⁰, ³¹, ³² If his children forsake My laws and don't obey them, then I will punish them, ³³ But I will never completely take away My lovingkindness from them, nor let My promise fail. ³⁴ No, I will not break My covenant; I will not take back one word of what I said. ³⁵, ³⁶ For I have sworn to David, (and a holy God can never lie), that his dynasty will go on forever, and his throne will continue to the end of time. ³⁷ It shall be eternal as the moon, My faithful witness in the sky!"

³⁸ Then why cast me off, rejected? Why be so angry with the one You chose as king? ³⁹ Have You renounced Your covenant with him? For You have thrown his crown in the dust. ⁴⁰ You have broken down the walls protecting him and laid in ruins every fort defending him. ⁴¹ Everyone who comes along has robbed him while his neighbors mock. ⁴² You have strengthened his enemies against him and made them rejoice. ⁴³ You have struck down his sword and refused to help him in battle. ⁴⁴ You have ended his

splendor and overturned his throne. ⁴⁵ You have made him old before his time and publicly disgraced him.

⁴⁶ O Jehovah, how long will this go on? Will You hide Yourself from me forever? How long will Your wrath burn like fire? ⁴⁷ Oh, remember how short You have made man's lifespan. Is it an empty, futile life You give the sons of men? ⁴⁸ No man can live forever. All will die. Who can rescue his life from the power of the grave?

⁴⁹ Lord, where is the love You used to have for me? Where is Your kindness that You promised to David with a faithful pledge? ⁵⁰ Lord, see how all the people are despising me. ⁵¹ Your enemies joke about me, the one You anointed as their king.

⁵² And yet — blessed be the Lord forever! Amen and Amen!

A Prayer of Moses, the Man of God

90 Lord, through all the generations You have been our home! ² Before the mountains were created, before the earth was formed, You are God without beginning or end.

³ You speak, and man turns back to dust. ⁴ A thousand years are but as yesterday to You! They are like a single hour! ⁵, ⁶ We glide along the tides of time as swiftly as a racing river, and vanish as quickly as a dream. We are like grass that is green in the morning but mowed down and withered before the evening shadows fall. ⁷ We die beneath Your anger; we are

overwhelmed by Your wrath. [8] You spread out our sins before You — our secret sins — and see them all. [9] No wonder the years are long and heavy here beneath Your wrath. All our days are filled with sighing.

[10]Seventy years are given us! And some may even live to 80. But even the best of these years are often emptiness and pain; soon they disappear, and we are gone. [11] Who can realize the terrors of Your anger? Which of us can fear You as he should?

[12] Teach us to number our days and recognize how few they are; help us to spend them as we should.

[13] O Jehovah, come and bless us! How long will You delay? Turn away Your anger from us. [14] Satisfy us in our earliest youth with Your lovingkindness, giving us constant joy to the end of our lives. [15] Give us gladness in proportion to our former misery! Replace the evil years with good. [16] Let us see Your miracles again; let our children see glorious things, the kind You used to do,

[17] And let the Lord our God favor us and give us success.

Proverbs for the Eighteenth Day

18 The selfish man quarrels against every sound principle of conduct by demanding his own way.

†

² A rebel doesn't care about the facts. All he wants to do is yell.

†

³ Sin brings disgrace.

†

⁴ A wise man's words express deep streams of thought.

†

⁵ It is wrong for a judge to favor the wicked and condemn the innocent.

†

⁶, ⁷ A fool gets into constant fights. His mouth is his undoing! His words endanger him.

†

⁸ What dainty morsels rumors are. They are eaten with great relish!

†

⁹ A lazy man is brother to the saboteur.

†

¹⁰ The Lord is a strong fortress. The godly run to Him and are safe.

¹¹ The rich man thinks of his wealth as an impregnable defense, a high wall of safety. What a dreamer!

†

¹² Pride ends in destruction; humility ends in honor.

†

¹³ What a shame — yes, how stupid! — to decide before knowing the facts!

†

¹⁴ A man's courage can sustain his broken body, but when courage dies, what hope is left?

†

¹⁵ The intelligent man is always open to new ideas. In fact, he looks for them.

†

¹⁶ A bribe does wonders: it will bring you before men of importance!

†

¹⁷ Any story sounds true until someone tells the other side and sets the record straight.

†

¹⁸ A coin toss ends arguments and settles disputes between powerful opponents.

†

¹⁹ It is harder to win back the friendship of an offended brother than to capture a fortified city. His anger shuts you out like iron bars.

†

²⁰ Ability to give wise advice satisfies like a good meal!

†

²¹ Those who love to talk will suffer the consequences. Men have died for saying the wrong thing!

²² The man who finds a wife finds a good thing; she is a blessing to him from the Lord.

†

²³ The poor man pleads and the rich man answers with insults.

†

²⁴ Some people are friends in name only. Others are closer than brothers.

I will be with him in trouble, and rescue him and honor him. ¹⁶ I will satisfy him with a full life and give him My salvation.

92 It is good to say, "Thank You" to the Lord, to sing praises to the God who is above all gods.

Psalms for the Nineteenth Day

91 We live within the shadow of the Almighty, sheltered by the God who is above all gods.
² This I declare, that He alone is my refuge, my place of safety; He is my God, and I am trusting Him.
³ For He rescues you from every trap, and protects you from the fatal plague. ⁴ He will shield you with His wings! They will shelter you. His faithful promises are your armor. ⁵ Now you don't need to be afraid of the dark any more, nor fear the dangers of the day;
⁶ Nor dread the plagues of darkness, nor disasters in the morning.

⁷ Though a thousand fall at my side, though ten thousand are dying around me, the evil will not touch me. ⁸ I will see how the wicked are punished but I will not share it. ⁹ For Jehovah is my refuge! I choose the God above all gods to shelter me. ¹⁰ How then can evil overtake me or any plague come near? ¹¹ For He orders His angels to protect you wherever you go.
¹² They will steady you with their hands to keep you from stumbling against the rocks on the trail. ¹³ You can safely meet a lion or step on poisonous snakes; yes, even trample them beneath your feet!

¹⁴ For the Lord says, "Because he loves Me, I will rescue him; I will make him great because he trusts in My name." ¹⁵ When he calls on Me I will answer;

I will be with him in trouble, and rescue him and honor him. [16] I will satisfy him with a full life and give him My salvation."

A Song To Sing On The Lord's Day

92 It is good to say, "Thank You" to the Lord, to sing praises to the God who is above all gods.

[2]Every morning tell Him, "Thank You for Your kindness," and every evening rejoice in all His faithfulness. [3] Sing His praises, accompanied by music from the harp and lute and lyre. [4] You have done so much for me, O Lord. No wonder I am glad! I sing for joy.

[5] O Lord, what miracles you do! And how deep are Your thoughts! [6] Unthinking people do not understand them! No fool can comprehend this: [7] That although the wicked flourish like weeds, there is only eternal destruction ahead of them. [8] But the Lord continues forever, exalted in the heavens, [9] While His enemies — all evil-doers — shall be scattered.

[10] But You have made me as strong as a wild bull. How refreshed I am by your blessings! [11] I have heard the doom of my enemies announced and seen them destroyed. [12] But the godly shall flourish like palm trees, and grow tall as the cedars of Lebanon. [13] For they are transplanted into the Lord's own garden, and are under His personal care. [14] Even in old age they will still produce fruit and be vital and green. [15] This honors the Lord, and exhibits His faithful care. He is my shelter. There is nothing but goodness in Him!

93 Jehovah is King! He is robed in majesty and strength. The world is His throne.

O Lord, you have reigned from prehistoric times, from the everlasting past. ³ The mighty oceans thunder Your praise. ⁴ You are mightier than all the breakers pounding on the seashores of the world! ⁵ Your royal decrees cannot be changed. Holiness is forever the keynote of Your reign.

94 Lord God, to whom vengeance belongs, let Your glory shine out. Arise and judge the earth; sentence the proud to the penalties they deserve. ³ Lord, how long shall the wicked be allowed to triumph and exult? ⁴ Hear their insolence! See their arrogance! How these men of evil boast! ⁵ See them oppressing Your people, O Lord, afflicting those You love. ⁶, ⁷ They murder widows, immigrants, and orphans, for "The Lord isn't looking," they say, "and besides, He doesn't care."

⁸ Fools! ⁹ Is God deaf and blind — He who makes ears and eyes? ¹⁰ He punishes the nations — won't He also punish you? He knows everything — doesn't He also know what you are doing?

¹¹ The Lord is fully aware of how limited and futile he thoughts of mankind are, ¹², ¹³ So He helps us by punishing us. This makes us follow His paths, and gives us respite from our enemies while God traps them and destroys them. ¹⁴ The Lord will not forsake His people, for they are His prize. ¹⁵ Judgment will again be just and all the upright will rejoice.

¹⁶ Who will protect me from the wicked? Who will be my shield? ¹⁷ I would have died unless the Lord had helped me. ¹⁸ I screamed, "I'm slipping, Lord!" and He was kind and saved me.

¹⁹ Lord, when doubts fill my mind, when my heart is in turmoil, quiet me and give me renewed hope and cheer. ²⁰ Will You permit a corrupt government to rule under Your protection — a government permitting wrong to defeat right? ²¹, ²² Do You approve of those who condemn the innocent to death? No! The Lord my God is my fortress — the mighty Rock where I can hide. ²³ God has made the sins of evil men to boomerang upon them! He will destroy them by their own plans! Jehovah our God will cut them off.

95 Oh, come, let us sing to the Lord! Give a joyous shout in honor of the Rock of our salvation!

² Come before Him with thankful hearts. Let us sing Him psalms of praise. ³ For the Lord is a great God, the great King of all gods. ⁴ He controls the formation of the depths of the earth and the mightiest mountains; all are His. ⁵ He made the sea and formed the land; they too are His. ⁶ Come, kneel before the Lord our Maker, ⁷ For He is our God. We are His sheep and He is our shepherd! Oh, that you would hear Him calling you today and come to Him!

⁸ Don't harden your hearts as Israel did in the wilderness at Meribah and Massah. ⁹ For there your fathers doubted Me, though they had seen so many of My miracles before. My patience was severely tried by their complaints. ¹⁰ "I watched them in disgust," the Lord God says. "They were a nation whose thoughts and heart were far away from Me. They refused to accept My laws. ¹¹ Therefore in mighty wrath I swore that they would never enter the Promised Land, the place of rest I planned for them."

Proverbs for the Nineteenth Day

19 Better be poor and honest than rich and dishonest.

†

² It is dangerous and sinful to rush into the unknown.

†

³ A man may ruin his chances by his own foolishness and then blame it on the Lord!

†

⁴ A wealthy man has many "friends"; the poor man has none left.

†

⁵ Punish false witnesses. Track down liars.

†

⁶ Many beg favors from a man who is generous; everyone is his friend!

†

⁷ A poor man's own brothers turn away from him in embarrassment; how much more his friends! He calls after them, but they are gone.

†

⁸ He who loves wisdom loves his own best interest and will be a success.

⁹ A false witness shall be punished and a liar shall be caught.

†

¹⁰ It doesn't seem right for a fool to succeed or for a slave to rule over princes!

†

¹¹ A wise man restrains his anger and overlooks insults. This is to his credit.

†

¹² The king's anger is as dangerous as a lion's. But his approval is as refreshing as the dew on grass.

†

¹³ A rebellious son is a calamity to his father, and a nagging wife annoys like constant dripping.

†

¹⁴ A father can give his sons homes and riches, but only the Lord can give them understanding wives.

†

¹⁵ A lazy man sleeps soundly — and goes hungry!

†

¹⁶ Keep the commandments and keep your life; despising them means death.

†

¹⁷ When you help the poor you are lending to the Lord — and He pays wonderful interest on your loan!

†

¹⁸ Discipline your son in his early years while there is hope. If you don't you will ruin his life.

†

¹⁹ A short-tempered man must bear his own penalty; you can't do much to help him. If you try once you must try a dozen times!

²⁰ Get all the advice you can and be wise the rest of your life.

†

²¹ Man proposes, but God disposes.

†

²² Kindness makes a man attractive. And it is better to be poor than dishonest.

†

²³ Reverence for God gives life, happiness, and protection from harm.

†

²⁴ Some men are so lazy they won't even feed themselves!

†

²⁵ Punish a mocker and others will learn from his example. Reprove a wise man and he will be the wiser.

†

²⁶ A son who mistreats his father or mother is a public disgrace.

†

²⁷ Stop listening to teaching that contradicts what you know is right.

†

²⁸ A worthless witness cares nothing for truth — he enjoys his sinning too much.

†

²⁹ Mockers and rebels shall be severely punished.

Psalms for the Twentieth Day

96 Sing a new song to the Lord! Sing it everywhere around the world! ² Sing out His praises! Bless His name. Each day tell someone that He saves.

³ Publish His glorious acts throughout the earth. Tell everyone about the amazing things He does. ⁴ For the Lord is great beyond description, and greatly to be praised. Worship only Him among the gods! ⁵ For the gods of other nations are merely idols, but our God made the heavens! ⁶ Honor and majesty surround Him; strength and beauty are in His Temple.

⁷ O nations of the world, confess that God alone is glorious and strong. ⁸ Give Him the glory He deserves! Bring your offering and come to worship Him. ⁹ Worship the Lord with the beauty of holy lives. Let the earth tremble before Him. ¹⁰ Tell the nations that Jehovah reigns! He rules the world. His power can never be overthrown. He will judge all nations fairly.

¹¹ Let the heavens be glad, the earth rejoice; let the vastness of the roaring seas demonstrate His glory. ¹² Praise Him for the growing fields, for they display His greatness. Let the trees of the forest rustle with

praise. [13] For the Lord is coming to judge the earth; He will judge the nations fairly and with truth!

97 Jehovah is King! Let all the earth rejoice! Tell the farthest islands to be glad.

[2] Clouds and darkness surround Him! Righteousness and justice are the foundation of His throne. [3] Fire goes forth before Him and burns up all His foes. [4] His lightning flashes out across the world. The earth sees and trembles. [5] The mountains melt like wax before the Lord of all the earth. [6] The heavens declare His perfect righteousness; every nation sees His glory.

[7] Let those who worship idols be disgraced — all who brag about their worthless gods — for every god must bow to Him! [8, 9] Jerusalem and all the cities of Judah have heard of Your justice, Lord, and are glad that You reign in majesty over the entire earth and are far greater than these other gods.

[10] The Lord loves those who hate evil; He protects the lives of His people, and rescues them from the wicked. [11] Light is sown for the godly and joy for the good. [12] May all who are godly be happy in the Lord and crown Him, our holy God.

98 Sing a new song to the Lord telling about His mighty deeds! For He has won a mighty victory by His power and holiness. [2, 3] He has announced this victory and revealed it to every nation by fulfilling His promise to be kind to Israel. The whole earth has seen God's salvation of His people. [4] That is why the earth breaks out in praise to God, and sings for utter joy!

⁵ Sing your praise accompanied by music from the harp. ⁶ Let the cornets and trumpets shout! Make a joyful symphony before the Lord, the King! ⁷ Let the sea in all its vastness roar with praise! Let the earth and all those living on it shout, "Glory to the Lord."

⁸, ⁹ Let the waves clap their hands in glee, and the hills sing out their songs of joy before the Lord, for He is coming to judge the world with perfect justice.

99 Jehovah is King! Let the nations tremble! He is enthroned upon the cherubim. Let the whole earth shake.

² Jehovah sits in majesty in Zion, supreme above all rulers of the earth. ³ Let them reverence Your great and holy name.

⁴ This mighty King is determined to give justice. Fairness is the touchstone of everything He does. He gives justice throughout Israel. ⁵ Exalt the Lord our holy God! Bow low before His feet.

⁶ When Moses and Aaron and Samuel, His prophet, cried to Him for help, He answered them. ⁷ He spoke to them from the pillar of cloud and they followed his instructions. ⁸ O Jehovah our God! You answered them and forgave their sins, yet punished them when they went wrong.

⁹ Exalt the Lord our God, and worship at His holy mountain in Jerusalem for He is holy.

100 Shout with joy before the Lord, O earth! ² Obey Him gladly; come before Him singing with joy.

³ Try to realize what this means — the Lord is God!

He made us — we are His people, the sheep of His pasture.

⁴ Go through His open gates with great thanksgiving; enter His courts with praise. Give thanks to Him and bless His name. ⁵ For the Lord is always good. He is always loving and kind, and His faithfulness goes on and on to each succeeding generation.

Proverbs for the Twentieth Day

20 Wine gives false courage; hard liquor leads to brawls; what fools men are to let it master them, making them reel drunkenly down the street!

†

² The king's fury is like that of a roaring lion; to rouse his anger is to risk your life.

†

³ It is an honor for a man to stay out of a fight. Only fools insist on quarreling.

†

⁴ If you won't plow in the cold you won't eat in the harvest.

†

⁵ Though good advice lies deep within a counselor's heart, the wise man will draw it out.

†

⁶ Most people will tell you what loyal friends they are, but are they telling the truth?

†

⁷ It is a wonderful heritage to have an honest father.

†

⁸ A king sitting as judge weighs all the evidence carefully, distinguishing the true from false.

⁹ Who can ever say, "I have cleansed my heart; I am sinless"?

†

¹⁰ The Lord despises every kind of cheating.

†

¹¹ The character of even a child can be known by the way he acts — whether what he does is pure and right.

†

¹² If you have good eyesight and good hearing, thank God who gave them to you.

†

¹³ If you love sleep, you will end in poverty. Stay awake, work hard, and there will be plenty to eat!

†

¹⁴ "Utterly worthless!" says the buyer as he haggles over the price. But afterwards he brags about his bargain!

†

¹⁵ Good sense is far more valuable than gold or precious jewels.

†

¹⁶ It is risky to make loans to strangers!

†

¹⁷ Some men enjoy cheating, but the cake they buy with such ill-gotten gain will turn to gravel in their mouths.

†

¹⁸ Don't go ahead with your plans without the advice of others; don't go to war until they agree.

†

¹⁹ Don't tell your secrets to a gossip unless you want them broadcast to the world.

²⁰ God puts out the light of the man who curses his father or mother.

†

²¹ A fortune can be made from cheating, but there is a curse that goes with it.

†

²² Don't repay evil for evil. Wait for the Lord to handle the matter.

†

²³ The Lord loathes all cheating and dishonesty.

†

²⁴ Since the Lord is directing our steps, why try to understand everything that happens along the way?

†

²⁵ It is foolish and rash to make a promise to the Lord before counting the cost.

†

²⁶ A wise king stamps out crime by severe punishment.

†

²⁷ A man's conscience is the Lord's searchlight exposing his hidden motives.

†

²⁸ If a king is kind, honest and fair, his kingdom stands secure.

†

²⁹ The glory of young men is their strength; of old men, their experience.

†

³⁰ Punishment that hurts chases evil from the heart.

Psalms for the Twenty-first day

101 I will sing about Your lovingkindness and Your justice, Lord. I will sing Your praises!

² I will try to walk a blameless path, but how I need Your help; especially in my own home, where I long to act as I should.

³ Help me to refuse the low and vulgar things; help me to abhor all crooked deals of every kind, to have no part in them. ⁴ I will reject all selfishness and stay away from every evil. ⁵ I will not tolerate any slander of my neighbors; I will not permit conceit and pride. ⁶ I will make the godly of the land my heroes, and invite them to my home. Those who are truly good shall be my examples. ⁷ But I will not allow those who deceive and lie to stay in my house. ⁸ My daily task will be to ferret out criminals and free the city of God from their grip.

A prayer when overwhelmed with trouble.

102 Lord, hear my prayer! Listen to my plea!

² Don't turn away from me in this time of my distress. Bend down Your ear and give me speedy answers, ³, ⁴ For my days disappear like smoke. My health is broken and my heart is sick; it is trampled like grass and is withered. My food is tasteless, and I

have lost my appetite. [5] I am reduced to skin and
bones because of all my groaning and despair. [6] I am
like a vulture in a far-off wilderness, or like an owl
alone in the desert. [7] I lie awake, lonely as a solitary
sparrow on the roof.

[8] My enemies taunt me day after day and curse at
me. [9, 10] I eat ashes instead of bread. My tears run
down into my drink because of Your anger against me,
because of Your wrath. For You have rejected me and
thrown me out. [11] My life is passing swiftly as the
evening shadows. I am withering like grass, [12] While
you, Lord, are a famous King forever. Your fame will
endure to every generation.

[13] I know that You will come and have mercy on
Jerusalem — and now is the time to pity her — the
time You promised help. [14] For Your people love
every stone in her walls and feel sympathy for every
grain of dust in her streets. [15] Now let the nations
and their rulers tremble before the Lord, before His
glory. [16] For Jehovah will rebuild Jerusalem! He will
appear in His glory!

[17] He will listen to the prayers of the destitute, for
He is never too busy to heed their requests. [18] I am
recording this so that future generations will also
praise the Lord for all that He has done. And a people
that shall be created shall praise the Lord. [19] Tell
them that God looked down from His Temple in
heaven, [20] And heard the groans of His people in
slavery — they were children of death — and released
them, [21, 22] So that multitudes would stream to the
Temple to praise Him, and His praises were sung
throughout the city of Jerusalem; and many rulers
throughout the earth came to worship Him.

²³ He has cut me down in middle life, shortening my days. ²⁴ But I cried to Him, "O God, You live forever and forever! Don't let me die half through my years!

²⁵ In ages past You laid the foundations of the earth, and made the heavens with Your hands! ²⁶ They shall perish, but You go on forever. They will grow old, like worn-out clothing, and You will change them as a man putting on a new shirt and throwing away the old one! ²⁷ But You Yourself never grow old. You are forever, and Your years never end.

²⁸ But our families will continue; generation after generation will be preserved by Your protection.

103 I bless the holy name of God with all my heart. ² Yes, I will bless the Lord and not forget the glorious things He does for me.

³ He forgives all my sins! He heals me! ⁴ He ransoms me from hell! He surrounds me with lovingkindness and tender mercies! ⁵ He fills my life with good things! My youth is renewed like the eagle's! ⁶ He gives justice to all who are treated unfairly. ⁷ He revealed His will and nature to Moses and the people of Israel.

⁸ He is merciful and tender toward those who don't deserve it; He is slow to get angry and full of kindness and love! ⁹ He never bears a grudge, nor remains angry forever. ¹⁰ He has not punished us as we deserve for all our sins, ¹¹ For His mercy towards those who fear and honor Him is as great as the height of the heavens above the earth. ¹² He has removed our sins as far away from us as the east is from the west. ¹³ He is like a father to us, tender and sympathetic

to those who reverence Him. ^{14} For He knows we are but dust, ^{15} And that our days are few and brief, like grass, like flowers, ^{16} Blown by the wind and gone forever.

$^{17,\ 18}$ But the lovingkindness of the Lord is from everlasting to everlasting, to those who reverence Him; His salvation is to children's children of those who are faithful to His covenant and remember to obey Him!

^{19} The Lord has made the heavens His throne; from there He rules over everything there is. ^{20} Bless the Lord, you mighty angels of His who carry out His orders, listening for each of His commands. ^{21} Yes, bless the Lord, you armies of His angels who serve Him constantly.

^{22} Let everything everywhere bless the Lord. And how I bless Him too!

Proverbs for the Twenty-first Day

21 Just as water is turned into irrigation ditches, so the Lord directs the king's thoughts. He turns them wherever He wants to.

†

² We can justify our every deed but God looks at our motives.

†

³ God is more pleased when we are just and fair than when we give Him gifts.

†

⁴ Pride, lust, and evil actions are all sin.

†

⁵ Steady plodding brings prosperity; hasty speculation brings poverty.

†

⁶ Dishonest gain will never last, so why take the risk?

†

⁷ Because the wicked are unfair, their violence boomerangs and destroys them.

†

⁸ A man is known by his actions; an evil man lives an evil life; a good man lives a godly life.

†

⁹ It is better to live in the corner of an attic than with a crabby woman in a lovely home.

¹⁰ An evil man loves to harm others; being a good neighbor is out of his line.

†

¹¹ The wise man learns by listening; the simpleton can learn only by seeing scorners punished.

†

¹² The godly learn by watching ruin overtake the wicked.

†

¹³ He who shuts his ears to the cries of the poor will be ignored in his own time of need.

†

¹⁴ An angry man is silenced by giving him a gift!

†

¹⁵ A good man loves justice, but it is a calamity to evil-doers.

†

¹⁶ The man who strays away from common sense will end up dead!

†

¹⁷ A man who loves pleasure becomes poor; wine and luxury are not the way to riches!

†

¹⁸ The wicked will finally lose; the righteous will finally win.

†

¹⁹ Better to live in the desert than with a quarrelsome, complaining woman.

†

²⁰ The wise man saves for the future, but the foolish man spends whatever he gets.

²¹ The man who tries to be good, loving and kind finds life, righteousness and honor.

†

²² The wise man conquers the strong man and levels his defenses.

†

²³ Keep your mouth closed and you'll stay out of trouble.

†

²⁴ Mockers are proud, haughty and arrogant.

†

²⁵, ²⁶ The lazy man longs for many things but his hands refuse to work. He is greedy to get, while the godly love to give!

†

²⁷ God loathes the gifts of evil men, especially if they are trying to bribe Him!

†

²⁸ A false witness must be punished; an honest witness is safe.

†

²⁹ An evil man is stubborn, but a godly man will reconsider.

†

³⁰ No one, regardless of how shrewd or well-advised he is, can stand against the Lord.

†

³¹ Go ahead and prepare for the conflict, but victory comes from God.

Psalms for the Twenty-second Day

104 I bless the Lord: O Lord my God, how great You are! You are robed with honor and with majesty and light! You stretched out the starry curtain of the heavens, ³ And hollowed out the surface of the earth to form the seas. The clouds are His chariots! He rides upon the wings of the wind! ⁴ The angels are His messengers — His servants of fire!

⁵ You bound the world together so that it would never fall apart. ⁶ You clothed the earth with floods of waters covering up the mountains. ⁷, ⁸ You spoke, and at the sound of Your shout the water collected into its vast ocean beds, and mountains rose and valleys sank to the levels You decreed. ⁹ And then You set a boundary for the seas, so that they would never again cover the earth.

¹⁰ He placed springs in the valleys, and streams that gush from the mountains. ¹¹ They gave water for all the animals to drink. There the wild donkeys quench their thirst, ¹² And the birds nest beside the streams and sing among the branches of the trees. ¹³ He sends rain upon the mountains and fills the earth with fruit. ¹⁴ The tender grass grows up at His command to feed the cattle, and there are fruit trees, vegetables and grain for man to cultivate, ¹⁵ And wine to make him glad, and olive oil as lotion for his skin, and bread to

give him strength. [16] The Lord planted the cedars of Lebanon. They are tall and flourishing. [17] There the birds make their nests, the storks in the firs. [18] High in the mountains are pastures for the wild goats; and rock-badgers burrow in among the rocks and find protection there.

[19] He assigned the moon to mark the months, and the sun to mark the days. [20] He sends the night and darkness, when all the forest folk come out. [21] Then the young lions roar for their food; but they are dependent on the Lord. [22] At dawn they slink back into their dens to rest, [23] And men go off to work until the evening shadows fall again. [24] O Lord, what a variety You have made! And in wisdom You have made them all! The earth is full of Your riches.

[25] There before me lies the mighty ocean, teeming with life of every kind, both great and small. [26] And look! See the ships! And over there, the whale You made to play in the sea! [27] Every one of these depends on You to give them daily food. [28] You supply it, and they gather it! You open wide Your hand to feed them and they are satisfied with all Your bountiful provision.

[29] But if You turn away from them, then all is lost. And when You gather up their breath, they die and turn again to dust.

[30] Then You send Your Spirit, and new life is born to replenish all the living of the earth. [31] Praise God forever! How He must rejoice in all His work! [32] The earth trembles at His glance; the mountains burst into flame at His touch.

³³ I will sing to the Lord as long as I live! I will praise God to my last breath! ³⁴ May He be pleased by all these thoughts about Him, for He is the source of all my joy. ³⁵ Let all sinners perish — all who refuse to praise Him. But I will praise Him. Hallelujah!

105 Thank the Lord for all the glorious things He does; proclaim them to the nations. ² Sing His praises and tell everyone about His miracles. ³ Glory in the Lord; O worshipers of God, rejoice.

⁴ Search for Him and for His strength, and keep on searching!

^{5, 6} Think of the mighty deeds He did for us, His chosen ones — descendants of God's servant Abraham, and of Jacob. Remember how He destroyed our enemies. ⁷ He is the Lord our God. His goodness is seen everywhere throughout the land. ^{8, 9} Though a thousand generations pass He never forgets His promise, His covenant with Abraham and Isaac, ^{10, 11} And confirmed with Jacob. This is His never-ending treaty with the people of Israel: *"I will give you the land of Canaan as your inheritance."* ¹² He said this when they were but few in number, very few, and were only visitors in Canaan. ¹³ Later they were dispersed among the nations, and were driven from one kingdom to another; ¹⁴ But through it all He would not let one thing be done to them apart from His decision. He destroyed many a king who tried! ¹⁵ "Touch not these chosen ones of Mine," He warned, "and do not hurt My prophets."

¹⁶ He called for a famine on the land of Canaan, cutting off its food supply. ¹⁷ Then He sent Joseph as a slave to Egypt to save His people from starvation.

[18] There in prison they hurt his feet with fetters, and placed his neck in an iron collar, [19] Until God's time finally came — how God tested his patience! [20] Then the king sent for him and set him free. [21] He was put in charge of all the king's possessions. [22] At his pleasure he could imprison the king's aides and teach the king's advisors.

[23] Then Jacob (Israel) arrived in Egypt and lived there with his sons. [24] In the years that followed, the people of Israel multiplied explosively, until they were a greater nation than their rulers. [25] At that point God turned the Egyptians against the Israeli; they hated and enslaved them.

[26] But God sent Moses as His representative, and Aaron with him, [27] To call down miracles of terror upon the land of Egypt. [28] They followed His instructions and He sent thick darkness through the land, [29] And turned the nation's water into blood, poisoning the fish. [30] Then frogs invaded in enormous numbers; they were found even in the king's private rooms. [31] When Moses spoke, the flies and other insects swarmed in vast clouds from one end of Egypt to the other. [32] Instead of rain He sent down murderous hail, and lightning flashes overwhelmed the nation. [33] Their grape vines and fig trees were ruined; all the trees lay broken on the ground. [34] He spoke, and hordes of locusts came, [35] And ate up everything green, destroying all the crops. [36] Then He killed the oldest child in each Egyptian home, their pride and joy — [37] And brought His people safely out from Egypt, loaded with silver and gold; there were no sick and feeble folk among them then. [38] Egypt was glad when they were gone, for the dread of them was great.

³⁹ He spread out a cloud above them to shield them from the burning sun, and gave them a pillar of flame at night to give them light. ⁴⁰ They asked for meat and He sent them quail, and gave them manna — bread from heaven. ⁴¹ He opened up a rock, and water gushed out to form a river through the dry and barren land; ⁴² For He remembered His sacred promises to Abraham His servant.

⁴³ So He brought His chosen ones singing into the Promised Land. ⁴⁴ He gave them the lands of the Gentiles, complete with their growing crops; they ate what others planted. ⁴⁵ This was done to make them faithful and obedient to His laws. Hallelujah!

Proverbs for the Twenty-second Day

22 If you must choose, take a good name rather than great riches; for to be held in loving esteem is better than silver and gold.

†

² The rich and the poor are alike before the Lord who made them all.

†

³ A prudent man foresees the difficulties ahead and prepares for them; the simpleton goes blindly on and suffers the consequences .

†

⁴ True humility and respect for the Lord lead a man to riches, honor and long life.

†

⁵ The rebel walks a thorny, treacherous road; the man who values his soul will stay away.

†

⁶ Teach a child to choose the right path, and when he is older he will remain upon it.

†

⁷ Just as the rich rule the poor, so the borrower is servant to the lender.

⁸ The unjust tyrant will reap disaster and his reign of terror shall end.

†

⁹ Happy is the generous man, the one who feeds the poor.

†

¹⁰ Throw out the mocker, and you will be rid of tension, fighting and quarrels.

†

¹¹ He who values grace and truth is the king's friend.

†

¹² The Lord preserves the upright but ruins the plans of the wicked.

†

¹³ The lazy man is full of excuses. "I can't go to work!" he says. "If I go outside I might meet a lion in the street and be killed!"

†

¹⁴ A prostitute is a dangerous trap; those cursed of God are caught in it.

†

¹⁵ A youngster's heart is filled with rebellion, but punishment will drive it out of him.

†

¹⁶ He who gains by oppressing the poor or by bribing the rich shall end in poverty.

†

¹⁷⁻²¹ Listen to this wise advice; follow it closely, for it will do you good, and you can pass it on to others: *Trust in the Lord.* In the past, haven't I been right? Then believe what I am telling you now, and share it with others.

^{22, 23} Don't rob the poor and sick! For the Lord is their defender. If you injure them He will punish You.

†

^{24, 25} Keep away from angry, short-tempered men, lest you learn to be like them and endanger your soul.

†

^{26, 27} Unless you have the extra cash on hand, don't countersign a note. Why risk everything you own? They'll even take your bed!

†

²⁸ Do not move the ancient boundary marks. That is stealing.

†

²⁹ Do you know a hard working man? He shall be successful and stand before kings!

Psalms for the Twenty-third Day

106 Hallelujah! Thank You, Lord! How good You are! Your love for us keeps growing. ² Who can ever list the glorious miracles of God? Who can ever praise Him half enough?

³ Happiness comes to those who are fair to others and are always just and good.

⁴ Remember me too, O Lord, while You are blessing and saving Your people. ⁵ Let me share in Your chosen ones' prosperity and rejoice in all their joys, and receive the glory You give to them.

⁶ Both we and our fathers have sinned so much. ⁷ They weren't impressed by the wonder of Your miracles in Egypt, and soon forgot Your many acts of kindness to them. Instead they rebelled against You at the Red Sea. ⁸ Even so You saved them — to defend the honor of Your name and demonstrate Your power to all the world. ⁹ You commanded the Red Sea to divide, forming a dry road across its bottom. Yes, as dry as any desert! ¹⁰ Thus You rescued them from their enemies. ¹¹ Then the water returned and covered the road and drowned their foes; not one survived.

¹² Then at last His people believed Him. Then they finally sang His praise.

¹³ Yet how quickly they forgot again! They wouldn't wait for Him to act, ¹⁴ But demanded better food, testing God's patience to the breaking point. ¹⁵ So He gave them their demands, but sent them leanness in their souls. ¹⁶ They were envious of Moses; yes, and Aaron, too, the man anointed by God as His priest. ¹⁷ Because of this the earth opened and swallowed Dathan, Abiram and his friends; ¹⁸ And fire fell from heaven to consume these wicked men. ¹⁹, ²⁰ For they preferred a statue of an ox that eats grass, to the glorious presence of God Himself. ²¹, ²² Thus they despised their Savior who had done such mighty miracles in Egypt and at the Sea. ²³ So the Lord declared He would destroy them. But Moses, His chosen one, stepped into the breach between the people and their God and begged Him to turn from His wrath, and not destroy them.

²⁴ They refused to enter the Promised Land, for they wouldn't believe His solemn oath to care for them. ²⁵ Instead, they pouted in their tents and mourned and despised His command. ²⁶ Therefore He swore that He would kill them in the wilderness ²⁷ And send their children away to distant lands as exiles. ²⁸ Then our fathers joined the worshipers of Baal at Peor and even offered sacrifices to the dead! ²⁹ With all these things they angered Him — and so a plague broke out upon them ³⁰ And continued until Phineas executed those whose sins had caused the plague to start. ³¹ (For this good deed Phineas will be remembered forever.)

³² At Meribah, too, Israel angered God, causing Moses serious trouble, ³³ For he became angry and spoke foolishly. ³⁴ Nor did Israel destroy the nations

in the land as God had told them to, [35] But mingled in among the heathen and learned their evil ways, [36] Sacrificing to their idols, and were led away from God. [37, 38] They even sacrificed their little children to the demons — the idols of Canaan — shedding innocent blood and polluting the land with murder. [39] Their evil deeds defiled them, for their love of idols was adultery in the sight of God. [40] That is why Jehovah's anger burned against His people, and He abhorred them. [41, 42] That is why He let the heathen nations crush them. They were ruled by those who hated them and oppressed by their enemies.

[43] Again and again He delivered them from their slavery, but they continued to rebel against Him, and were finally destroyed by their sin. [44] Yet, even so, He listened to their cries and heeded their distress; [45] He remembered His promises to them and relented because of His great love, [46] And caused even their enemies who captured them to pity them.

[47] O Lord God, save us! Regather us from the nations so we can thank Your holy name and rejoice and praise You.

[48] Blessed be the Lord, the God of Israel, from everlasting to everlasting. Let all the people say, "Amen!" Hallelujah!

107 Say "Thank You" to the Lord for being so good, for always being so loving and kind. [2] Has the Lord redeemed You? Then speak out! Tell others He has saved you from your enemies.

[3] He brought the exiles back from the farthest corners of the earth. [4] They were wandering homeless in the desert, [5] Hungry and thirsty and faint.

⁶ "Lord, help!" they cried, and He did! ⁷ He led them straight to safety and a place to live. ⁸ Oh, that these men would praise the Lord for His lovingkindness, and for all of His wonderful deeds! ⁹ For He satisfies the thirsty soul and fills the hungry soul with good.

¹⁰ Who are these who sit in darkness, in the shadow of death, crushed by misery and slavery? ¹¹ They rebelled against the Lord, scorning Him who is the God above all gods. ¹² That is why He broke them with hard labor; they fell and none could help them rise again. ¹³ Then they cried to the Lord in their troubles, and He rescued them! ¹⁴ He led them from the darkness and shadow of death and snapped their chains! ¹⁵ Oh, that these men would praise the Lord for His lovingkindness and for all of His wonderful deeds! ¹⁶ For He broke down their prison gates of brass and cut apart their iron bars.

¹⁷ Others, the fools, were ill because of their sinful ways. ¹⁸ Their appetites were gone and death was near. ¹⁹ Then they cried to the Lord in their troubles, and He helped them and delivered them. ²⁰ He spoke, and they were healed — snatched from the door of death. ²¹ Oh, that these men would praise the Lord for His lovingkindness and for all of His wonderful deeds! ²² Let them tell Him "Thank You" as their sacrifice, and sing about His glorious deeds.

²³ And then there are the sailors sailing the seven seas, plying the trade routes of the world. ²⁴ They, too, observe the power of God in action. ²⁵ He calls to the storm winds; the waves rise high. ²⁶ Their ships are tossed to the heavens and sink again to the depths; the sailors cringe in terror. ²⁷ They reel and stagger

like drunkards and are at their wit's end. ²⁸ Then they cry to the Lord in their trouble, and He saves them! ²⁹ He calms the storm and stills the waves. ³⁰ What a blessing is that stillness, as He brings them safely into harbor! ³¹ Oh, that these men would praise the Lord for His lovingkindness for all of His wonderful deeds! ³² Let them praise Him publicly before the congregation, and before the leaders of the nation.

³³ He dries up rivers, ³⁴ And turns the good land of the wicked into deserts of salt. ³⁵ Again, He turns deserts into fertile, watered valleys! ³⁶ He brings the hungry to settle there and build their cities, ³⁷ To sow their fields and plant their vineyards, and reap their bumper crops! ³⁸ How He blesses them! They raise big families there, and many cattle!

³⁹ But others become poor through oppression, trouble and sorrow. ⁴⁰ For God pours contempt upon the haughty and causes princes to wander among ruins; ⁴¹ But He rescues the poor who are godly and gives them many children and much prosperity. ⁴² Good men everywhere will see it and be glad, while evil men are stricken silent.

⁴³ Listen, if you are wise, to what I am saying. Think about the lovingkindness of the Lord!

Proverbs for the Twenty-third Day

23 When dining with a rich man, be on your guard and don't stuff yourself, though it all tastes so good; for he is trying to bribe you, and no good is going to come of his invitation.

†

⁴, ⁵ Don't weary yourself trying to get rich. Why waste your time? For riches can disappear as though they had the wings of a bird!

†

⁶⁻⁸ Don't become obligated to evil men; don't long for their favors and gifts. Their kindness is a trick; they want to use you as their pawn. The delicious food they serve will turn sour in your stomach and you will vomit it, and have to take back your words of appreciation for their "kindness."

†

⁹ Don't waste your breath on a rebel. He will despise the wisest advice.

†

¹⁰, ¹¹ Don't steal the land of defenseless orphans by moving their ancient boundary marks, for their Redeemer is strong; He Himself will accuse you.

†

¹² Don't refuse to accept criticism; get all the help you can.

13, 14 Don't fail to correct your children; discipline won't hurt them! They won't die if you use a stick on them! Punishment will keep them out of hell.

†

15, 16 My son, how I will rejoice if you become a man of common sense. Yes, my heart will thrill to your thoughtful, wise words.

†

17, 18 Don't envy evil men but continue to reverence the Lord all the time, for surely you have a wonderful future ahead of you. There is hope for you yet!

†

19-21 O my son, be wise and stay in God's paths; don't carouse with drunkards and gluttons, for they are on their way to poverty. And remember that too much sleep clothes a man with rags. 22 Listen to your father's advice and don't despise an old mother's experience. 23 Get the facts at any price, and hold on tightly to all the good sense you can get. 24, 25 The father of a godly man has cause for joy — what pleasure a wise son is! So give your parents joy!

†

26-28 O my son, trust my advice — stay away from prostitutes. For a prostitute is a deep and narrow grave. Like a robber, she waits for her victims as one after another become unfaithful to their wives.

†

29, 30 Whose heart is filled with anguish and sorrow? Who is always fighting and quarreling? Who is the man with bloodshot eyes and many wounds? It is the one who spends long hours in the taverns, trying out new mixtures. 31 Don't let the sparkle and the smooth taste of strong wine deceive you.

³² For in the end it bites like a poisonous serpent; it stings like an adder.

†

³³ You will see hallucinations and have delirium tremens, and you will say foolish, silly things that would embarrass you no end when sober. ³⁴ You will stagger like a sailor tossed at sea, clinging to a swaying mast. ³⁵ And afterwards you will say, "I didn't even know it when they beat me up . . . Let's go and have another drink!"

Psalms for the Twenty-fourth Day

108 O, God, my heart is ready to praise You! I will sing and rejoice before You.

² Wake up, O harp and lyre! We will meet the dawn with song. ³ I will praise You everywhere around the world, in every nation. ⁴ For Your lovingkindness is great beyond measure, high as the heavens! Your faithfulness reaches the skies! ⁵ Your glory is far more vast than the heavens! It towers above the earth. ⁶ Hear the cry of Your beloved child — come with mighty power and rescue me.

⁷ God has given sacred promises; no wonder I exult! He has promised to give us all the land of Shechem, and also Succoth Valley! ⁸ "Gilead is Mine to give to you," He says, "and Manasseh as well; the land of Ephraim is the helmet on My head. Judah is My scepter. ⁹ But Moab and Edom are despised; and I will shout in triumph over the Philistines." ¹⁰ Who but God can give me strength to conquer these fortified cities? Who else can lead me into Edom?

¹¹ Lord, have You thrown us away? Have You deserted our army? ¹² Oh, help us fight against our enemies, for men are useless allies. ¹³ But with the help of God we shall do mighty acts of valor! For He treads down our foes.

109 O God of my praise, don't stand silent and aloof ² While the wicked slander me and tell their lies. ³ They have no reason to hate and fight me, yet they do! ⁴ I love them, but even while I am praying for them, they are trying to destroy me. ⁵ They return evil for good, and hatred for love!

⁶ Show him how it feels! Let lies be told about him, and bring him to court before an unfair judge. ⁷ When his case is called for judgment, let him be pronounced guilty! Count his prayers as sins! ⁸ Let his years be few and brief; let others step forward to replace him. ⁹, ¹⁰ May his children become fatherless and his wife a widow, and be evicted from the ruins of their home. ¹¹ May creditors seize his entire estate and strangers take all he has earned. ¹², ¹³ Let no one be kind to him; let no one pity his fatherless children. May they die. May his family name be blotted out in a single generation. ¹⁴ Punish the sins of his father and mother. Don't overlook them. ¹⁵ Think constantly about the evil things he has done, and cut off his name from the memory of man.

¹⁶ For he refused all kindness to others, and persecuted those in need, and hounded brokenhearted ones to death. ¹⁷ He loved to curse others; now You curse him. He never blessed others; now don't You bless him. ¹⁸ Cursing is as much a part of him as his clothing, or as the water he drinks, or the rich food he eats! ¹⁹ Now may those curses return and cling to him like his clothing or his belt. ²⁰ This is the Lord's punishment upon my enemies who tell lies about me and threaten me with death.

²¹ But as for me, O Lord, deal with me as Your child, as one who bears Your name! Because You are so kind, O Lord, deliver me.

^{22, 23} I am slipping down the hill to death; I am shaken off from life as easily as a man brushes a grasshopper from his arm. ²⁴ My knees are weak from fasting and I am skin and bones. ²⁵ I am a symbol of failure to all mankind; when they see me they shake their heads.

²⁶ Help me, O Lord my God! Save me because You are loving and kind. ²⁷ Do it publicly, so all will see that You Yourself have done it. ²⁸ Then let them curse me if they like — I won't mind that if You are blessing me! For then all their efforts to destroy me will fail, and I shall go right on rejoicing!

²⁹ Make them fail in everything they do. Clothe them with disgrace. ³⁰ But I will give repeated thanks to the Lord, praising Him to everyone. ³¹ For He stands beside the poor and hungry to save them from their enemies.

110 Jehovah said to my Lord the Messiah, "Rule as My regent — I will subdue Your enemies and make them bow low before You."

² Jehovah has established Your throne in Jerusalem to rule over Your enemies. ³ In that day of Your power Your people shall come to You willingly, dressed in holy altar robes. And Your strength shall be renewed day by day like morning dew. ⁴ Jehovah has taken oath, and will not rescind His vow, that You are a priest forever like Melchizedek. ⁵ God stands beside You to protect You. He will strike down many kings in the day of His anger. ⁶ He will punish the nations, and fill them with their dead. He will crush many heads. ⁷ But You Yourself shall be refreshed from springs along the way.

111 Hallelujah! I want to express publicly before His people my heartfelt thanks to God for His mighty miracles! All who are thankful should ponder them with me. ³ For His miracles demonstrate His honor, majesty, and eternal goodness.

⁴ Who can forget the wonders He performs — deeds of mercy and of grace? ⁵ He gives food to those who trust Him; He never forgets His promises! ⁶ He has shown His great power to His people by giving them the land of Israel, though it was the home of many nations living there. ⁷ All He does is just and good, and all His laws are right, ⁸ For they are formed from truth and goodness, and stand firm forever. ⁹ He has paid a full ransom for His people; now they are always free to come to God (what a holy, awe-inspiring name that is).

¹⁰How can men be wise? The only way to begin is by reverence for God. For growth in wisdom comes from obeying His laws. Praise His name forever.

Proverbs for the Twenty-fourth Day

24 Don't envy godless men; don't even enjoy their company. ² For they spend their days plotting violence and cheating.

†

³, ⁴ Any enterprise is built by wise planning, becomes strong through common sense, and profits wonderfully by keeping abreast of the facts.

†

⁵ A wise man is mightier than a strong man. Wisdom is mightier than strength.

†

⁶ Don't go to war without wise guidance; there is safety in many counselors.

†

⁷ Wisdom is too much for a rebel. He'll not be chosen as a counselor!

†

⁸ To plan evil is as wrong as doing it.

†

⁹ The rebel's schemes are sinful, and the mocker is the scourge of all mankind.

†

¹⁰ You are a poor specimen if you can't stand the pressure of adversity.

11, 12 Rescue those who are unjustly sentenced to death; don't stand back and let them die. Don't try to disclaim responsibility by saying you didn't know about it. For God, who knows all hearts, knows yours, and He knows you knew! And He will reward everyone according to his deeds.

†

13, 14 My son, honey whets the appetite, and so does wisdom! When you enjoy becoming wise, there is hope for you! A bright future lies ahead!

†

15, 16 O evil man, leave the upright man alone, and quit trying to cheat him out of his rights. Don't you know that this good man, though you trip him up seven times, will each time rise again? But one calamity is enough to lay you low.

†

17 Do not rejoice when your enemy meets trouble. Let there be no gladness when he falls — 18 For the Lord may be displeased with you and stop punishing him!

†

19, 20 Don't envy the wicked. Don't covet his riches. For the evil man has no future; his light will be snuffed out.

†

21, 22 My son, watch your step before the Lord and the king, and don't associate with radicals. For you will go down with them to sudden disaster, and who knows where it all will end?

†

Here are some additional proverbs:

²³ It is wrong to sentence the poor, and let the rich go free. ²⁴ He who says to the wicked, "You are innocent," shall be cursed by many people of many nations; ²⁵ But blessings shall be showered on those who rebuke sin fearlessly.

†

²⁶ It is an honor to receive a frank reply.

†

²⁷ Develop your business first before building your house.

†

^{28, 29} Don't testify spitefully against an innocent neighbor. Why lie about him? Don't say, "Now I can pay him back for all his meanness to me!"

†

^{30, 31} I walked by the field of a certain lazy fellow and saw that it was overgrown with thorns, and covered with weeds; and its walls were broken down. ³² Then, as I looked, I learned this lesson:

³³ "A little extra sleep,
    A little more slumber,
    A little folding of the hands to rest" —
³⁴ Means that poverty will break in upon you suddenly like a robber, and violently like a bandit.

Psalms for the Twenty-fifth Day

112 Praise the Lord! For all who fear God and trust in Him are blessed beyond expression. Yes, happy is the man who delights in doing His commands.

² His children shall be honored everywhere, for good men's sons have a special heritage. ³ He himself shall be wealthy, and his good deeds will never be forgotten. ⁴ When darkness overtakes him, light will come bursting in. He is kind and merciful — ⁵ And all goes well for the generous man who conducts his business fairly.

⁶ Such a man will not be overthrown by evil circumstances. God's constant care of him will make a deep impression on all who see it. ⁷ He does not fear bad news, nor live in dread of what may happen. For he is settled in his mind that Jehovah will take care of him. ⁸ That is why he is not afraid, but can calmly face his foes. ⁹ He gives generously to those in need. His deeds will never be forgotten. He shall have influence and honor.

¹⁰ Evil-minded men will be infuriated when they see all this; they will gnash their teeth in anger and slink away, their hopes thwarted.

113 Hallelujah! O servants of Jehovah, praise His name. ² Blessed is His name forever and forever.

³ Praise Him from sunrise to sunset! ⁴ For He is high above the nations; His glory is far greater than the heavens.

⁵ Who can be compared with God enthroned on high? ⁶ Far below Him are the heavens and the earth; He stoops to look, ⁷ And lifts the poor from the dirt, and the hungry from the garbage dump, ⁸ And sets them among princes! ⁹ He gives children to the childless wife, so that she becomes a happy mother.

Hallelujah! Praise the Lord!

114 Long ago when the Israeli escaped from Egypt, from that land of foreign tongue, ² Then the lands of Judah and of Israel became God's new home and kingdom.

³ The Red Sea saw them coming and quickly broke apart before them! The Jordan River opened up a path for them to cross! ⁴ The mountains skipped like rams, the little hills like lambs! ⁵ What's wrong, Red Sea, that made you cut yourself in two? What happened, Jordan River, to your waters? Why were they held back? ⁶ Why, mountains, did you skip like rams? Why, little hills, like lambs?

⁷ Tremble, O earth, at the presence of the Lord, the God of Jacob. ⁸ For He caused gushing streams to burst from flinty rock.

115 Glorify Your name, not ours O Lord! Cause everyone to praise Your lovingkindness and Your truth. ² Why let the nations say, "Their God is dead!"

³ For He is in the heavens, and does as He wishes.

⁴ Their gods are merely man-made things of silver and of gold. ⁵ They can't talk or see, despite their eyes and mouths! ⁶ Nor can they hear, nor smell, ⁷ Nor use their hands or feet! Nor speak! ⁸ And those who make and worship them are just as foolish as their idols are.

⁹ O Israel, trust the Lord! He is your helper. He is your shield. ¹⁰ O priests of Aaron, trust the Lord! He is your helper; He is your shield. ¹¹ All of you His people, trust in Him. He is your helper; He is your shield.

¹² Jehovah is constantly thinking about us and He will surely bless us! He will bless the people of Israel and the priests of Aaron, ¹³ And all, both great and small, who reverence Him.

¹⁴ May the Lord bless you richly both you and your children. ¹⁵ Yes, Jehovah who made heaven and earth will personally bless you! ¹⁶ The heavens belong to the Lord, but He has given the earth to all mankind.

¹⁷ The dead cannot sing praises to Jehovah here on earth, ¹⁸ But we can! We praise Him forever! Hallelujah! Praise the Lord!

116 I love the Lord because He hears my prayers and answers them. ² Because He bends down and listens, I will pray as long as I breathe!

³ Death stared me in the face — I was frightened and sad. ⁴ Then I cried, "Lord, save me!" ⁵ How kind He is! How good He is! So merciful, this God of ours! ⁶ The Lord protects the simple and the childlike: I was facing death and then He saved me. ⁷ Now

I can relax. For the Lord has done this wonderful miracle for me. [8] He has saved me from death, my eyes from tears, my feet from stumbling. [9] I shall live! Yes, in His presence — here on earth!

[10, 11] In my discouragement I thought, "They are lying when they say I will recover." [12] But now what can I offer Jehovah for all He has done for me? [13] I will bring Him an offering of wine and praise His name. [14] I will publicly bring Him the sacrifice I vowed I would. [15] His loved ones are very precious to Him and He does not lightly let them die.

[16] O Lord, You have freed me from my bonds and I will serve you forever. [17] I will worship You and offer You a sacrifice of thanksgiving. [18, 19] Here in the courts of the Temple in Jerusalem, before all the people, I will pay everything I vowed to the Lord. Praise the Lord.

117 Praise the Lord, all nations everywhere. Laud Him, all the peoples of the earth. [2] For He loves us very dearly, and His truth endures. Praise the Lord.

118 Oh, thank the Lord, for He's so good! His lovingkindness is forever.

[2] Let the congregation of Israel praise Him with these same words: "His lovingkindness is forever." [3] And let the priests of Aaron chant, "His lovingkindness is forever." [4] Let the Gentile converts chant, "His lovingkindness is forever."

[5] In my distress I prayed to the Lord and He answered me and rescued me. [6] He is for me! How can I be afraid? What can mere man do to me? [7] The Lord is on my side, He will help me. Let those who hate me beware.

⁸ It is better to trust the Lord than to put confidence in men. ⁹ It is better to take refuge in Him than in the mightiest king!

¹⁰ Though all the nations of the world attack me, I will march out behind His banner and destroy them. ¹¹ Yes, they surround and attack me; but with His flag flying above me I will cut them off. ¹² They swarm around me like bees; they blaze against me like a roaring flame. Yet beneath His flag I shall destroy them. ¹³ You did your best to kill me, O my enemy, but the Lord helped me. ¹⁴ He is my strength and song in the heat of battle, and now He has given me the victory. ¹⁵, ¹⁶ Songs of joy at the news of our rescue are sung in the homes of the godly. The strong arm of the Lord has done glorious things! ¹⁷ I shall not die, but live to tell of all His deeds. ¹⁸ The Lord has punished me, but not handed me over to Death.

¹⁹ Open the gates of the Temple — I will go in and give Him my thanks. ²⁰ Those gates are the way into the presence of the Lord, and the godly enter there. ²¹ O Lord, thank you so much for answering my prayer and saving me.

²² The stone rejected by the builders has now become the capstone of the arch! ²³ This is the Lord's doing, and it is marvelous to see! ²⁴ This is the day the Lord has made. We will rejoice and be glad in it. ²⁵ O Lord, please help us. Save us. Give us success. ²⁶ Blessed is the One who is coming, the One sent by the Lord. We bless You from the Temple.

²⁷, ²⁸ Jehovah God is our light. I present to Him my sacrifice upon the altar, for You are my God, and I shall give You this thanks and this praise. ²⁹ Oh, give thanks to the Lord, for He is so good! For His lovingkindness is forever.

Proverbs for the Twenty-fifth Day

These proverbs of Solomon were discovered and copied by the aides of King Hezekiah of Judah:

25 [2, 3] It is God's privilege to conceal things, and the king's privilege to discover and invent. You cannot understand the height of heaven, the size of the earth or all that goes on in the king's mind!

†

[4, 5] When you remove dross from silver, you have sterling ready for the silversmith. When you remove corrupt men from the king's court, his reign will be just and fair.

†

[6, 7] Don't demand an audience with the king as though you were some powerful prince. It is better to wait for an invitation rather than to be sent back to the end of the line, publicly disgraced!

†

[8, 9, 10] Don't be hot-headed and rush to court! You may start something you can't finish and go down before your neighbor in shameful defeat. So discuss the matter with him privately. Don't tell anyone else, lest he accuse you of slander and you can't withdraw what you said.

†

[11] Timely advice is as lovely as golden apples in a silver basket.

¹² It is a badge of honor to accept valid criticism.

†

¹³ A faithful employee is as refreshing as a cool day in the hot summertime.

†

¹⁴ One who doesn't give the gift he promised is like a cloud blowing over a desert without dropping any rain.

†

¹⁵ Be patient and you will finally win, for a soft tongue can break hard bones.

†

¹⁶ Do you like honey? Don't eat too much of it, or it will make you sick!

†

¹⁷ Don't visit your neighbor too often, or you will outwear your welcome!

†

¹⁸ Telling lies about someone is as harmful as hitting him with an axe, or wounding him with a sword, or shooting him with a sharp arrow.

†

¹⁹ Putting confidence in an unreliable man is like chewing with a sore tooth, or trying to run on a broken foot.

†

²⁰ Being happy-go-lucky around a person whose heart is heavy is as bad as stealing his jacket in cold weather, or rubbing salt in his wounds.

†

²¹, ²² If your enemy is hungry, give him food! If he is thirsty, give him something to drink! This will make him feel ashamed of himself, and God will reward you.

²³ As surely as a wind from the north brings cold, just as surely a retort causes anger!

†

²⁴ It is better to live in a corner of an attic than in a beautiful home with a cranky, quarrelsome woman.

†

²⁵ Good news from far away is like cold water to the thirsty.

†

²⁶ If a godly man compromises with the wicked, it is like polluting a fountain or muddying a spring.

†

²⁷ Just as it is harmful to eat too much honey, so also it is bad for men to think about all the honors they deserve!

†

²⁸ A man without self-control is as defenseless as a city with broken-down walls.

²³ As surely as a wind from the north brings cold, just as surely a secret causes anger.

†

²⁴ It is better to live in a corner of an attic than in a beautiful home with a cranky, quarrelsome woman.

†

²⁵ Good news from far away is like cold water to the thirsty.

†

²⁶ If a godly man compromises with the wicked, it is like polluting a fountain or muddying a spring.

†

²⁷ Just as it is harmful to eat too much honey, so also is it bad for men to think about all the honors they deserve.

†

²⁸ A man without self-control is as defenseless as a city with broken-down walls.

Psalms for the Twenty-sixth Day

119 Happy are all who perfectly follow the laws of God. ² Happy are all who search for God, and always do His will, ³ Rejecting compromise with evil, and walking only in His paths. ⁴ You have given us Your laws to obey — ⁵ Oh, how I want to follow them consistently. ⁶ Then I will not be disgraced, for I will have a clean record.

⁷ After You have corrected me I will thank You by living as I should! ⁸ I *will* obey! Oh, don't forsake me and let me slip back into sin again.

⁹ How can a young man stay pure? By reading Your Word and following its rules. ¹⁰ I have tried my best to find You — don't let me wander off from Your instructions. ¹¹ I have thought much about Your words, and stored them in my heart so that they would hold me back from sin.

¹² Blessed Lord, teach me Your rules. ¹³ I have recited Your laws, ¹⁴ And rejoiced in them more than in riches. ¹⁵ I will meditate upon them and give them my full respect. ¹⁶ I will delight in them and not forget them.

¹⁷ Bless me with life so that I can continue to obey You. ¹⁸ Open my eyes to see wonderful things in Your Word. ¹⁹ I am but a pilgrim here on earth: how

I need a map — and Your commands are my chart and guide. [20] I long for Your instructions more than I can tell.

[21] You rebuke those cursed proud ones who refuse Your commands — [22] Don't let them scorn me for obeying You. [23] For even princes sit and talk against me, but I will continue in Your plans. [24] Your laws are both my light and my counselors.

[25] I am completely discouraged — I lie in the dust. Revive me by Your Word. [26] I told You my plans and You replied. Now give me Your instructions. [27] Make me understand what You want; for then I shall see Your miracles.

[28] I weep with grief; my heart is heavy with sorrow; encourage and cheer me with Your words. [29, 30] Keep me far from every wrong; help me, undeserving as I am, to obey Your laws, for I have chosen to do right. [31] I cling to Your commands and follow them as closely as I can. Lord, don't let me make a mess of things. [32] If You will only help me to want Your will, then I will follow Your laws even more closely.

[33, 34] Just tell me what to do and I will do it, Lord. As long as I live I'll wholeheartedly obey. [35] Make me walk along the right paths for I know how delightful they really are.

[36] Help me to prefer obedience to making money! [37] Turn me away from wanting any other plan than Yours. Revive my heart toward You. [38] Reassure me that Your promises are for me; for I trust and revere You.

³⁹ How I dread being mocked for obeying; for Your laws are right and good. ^{40, 41, 42} I long to obey them! Therefore in fairness renew my life, for this was Your promise — yes, Lord, to save me! Now spare me this kindness and love. Then I will have an answer for those who taunt me, for I trust Your promises.

⁴³ May I never forget Your words; for they are my only hope. ^{44, 45, 46} Therefore I will keep on obeying You forever and forever, free within the limits of Your laws. I will speak to kings about their value, and they will listen with interest and respect.

⁴⁷ How I love Your laws! How I enjoy Your commands! ⁴⁸ "Come, come to me," I call to them, for I love them and will let them fill my life.

^{49, 50} Never forget Your promises to me Your servant; for they are my only hope. They give me strength in all my troubles; how they refresh and revive me! ⁵¹ Proud men hold me in contempt for obedience to God, but I stand unmoved. ⁵² From my earliest youth I have tried to obey You; Your Word has been my comfort.

⁵³ I am very angry with those who spurn Your commands. ⁵⁴ For these laws of Yours have been my source of joy and singing through all these years of my earthly pilgrimage. ⁵⁵ I obey them even at night and keep my thoughts, O Lord, on You. ⁵⁶ What a blessing this has been to me — to constantly obey.

⁵⁷ Jehovah is mine! And I promise to obey! ⁵⁸ With all my heart I want Your blessings. Be merciful just as You promised. ^{59, 60} I thought about the wrong direction in which I was headed, and turned around and came running back to You. ⁶¹ Evil men

have tried to drag me into sin, but I am firmly anchored to Your laws.

⁶² At midnight I will rise to give my thanks to You for Your good laws. ⁶³ Anyone is my brother who fears and trusts the Lord and obeys Him. ⁶⁴ O Lord, the earth is full of Your lovingkindness! Teach me Your good paths.

⁶⁵ Lord, I am overflowing with Your blessings, just as You promised! ⁶⁶ Now teach me good judgment as well as knowledge! For Your laws are my guide. ⁶⁷ I used to wander off until You punished me; now I closely follow all You say. ⁶⁸ You are good and do only good; make me follow Your lead!

⁶⁹ Proud men have made up lies about me, but the truth is that I obey Your laws with all my heart. ⁷⁰ Their minds are dull and stupid, but I have sense enough to follow You.

⁷¹, ⁷² The punishment You gave me was the best thing that could have happened to me, for it taught me to pay attention to Your laws. They are more valuable to me than millions in silver and gold!

⁷³ You made my body, Lord; now give me sense to heed Your laws. ⁷⁴ All those who fear and trust in You will welcome me because I too am trusting in Your Word.

⁷⁵, ⁷⁶, ⁷⁷ I know, O Lord, that Your decisions are right and that Your punishment was right and did me good. Now let Your lovingkindness comfort me, just as You promised. Surround me with Your tender mercies, that I may live. For Your law is my delight.

⁷⁸ Let the proud be disgraced, for they have cut me down with all their lies. But I will concentrate my thoughts upon Your laws.

⁷⁹ Let all others join me, who trust and fear You, and we will discuss Your laws. ⁸⁰ Help me to love Your every wish; then I will never have to be ashamed of myself!

⁸¹ I faint for Your salvation; but I expect Your help, for You have promised it. ⁸² My eyes are straining to see Your promises come true. When will You comfort me with Your help? ⁸³ I am shriveled like a wineskin in the smoke, exhausted with waiting. But still I cling to Your laws and obey them. ⁸⁴ How long must I wait before You punish those who persecute me? ⁸⁵, ⁸⁶ These proud men who hate Your truth and laws have dug deep pits for me to fall in. Their lies have brought me into deep trouble. Help me, for You love only truth. ⁸⁷ They had almost finished me off, yet I refused to yield and disobey Your laws. ⁸⁸ In Your kindness, spare my life; then I can continue to obey You.

⁸⁹ Forever, O Lord, Your Word stands firm in heaven. ⁹⁰, ⁹¹ Your faithfulness extends to every generation, like the earth You created; it endures by Your decree, for everything serves Your plans.

⁹² I would have despaired and perished unless Your laws had been my deepest delight. ⁹³ I will never lay aside Your laws, for You have used them to restore my joy and health. ⁹⁴ I am Yours! Save me! For I have tried to live according to Your desires. ⁹⁵ Though the wicked hide along the way to kill me, I will quietly keep my mind upon Your promises.

⁹⁶ Nothing is perfect except Your words. ⁹⁷ Oh, how I love them. I think about them all day long. ⁹⁸ They make me wiser than my enemies, because they are my constant guide. ⁹⁹ Yes, wiser than my teachers; for I am ever thinking of Your rules. ¹⁰⁰ They make me even wiser than the aged.

¹⁰¹ I have refused to walk the paths of evil for I will remain obedient to Your Word. ¹⁰², ¹⁰³ No, I haven't turned away from what You taught me: Your words are sweeter than honey. ¹⁰⁴ And since only Your rules can give me wisdom and understanding, no wonder I hate every false teaching.

¹⁰⁵ Your words are a flashlight to light the path ahead of me, and keep me from stumbling. ¹⁰⁶ I've said it once and I'll say it again and again: I will obey these wonderful laws of Yours.

¹⁰⁷ I am close to death at the hands of my enemies; oh, give me back my life again, just as You promised me. ¹⁰⁸ Accept my grateful thanks and teach me Your desires. ¹⁰⁹ My life hangs in the balance, but I will not give up obedience to Your laws. ¹¹⁰ The wicked have set their traps for me along Your path, but I will not turn aside. ¹¹¹ Your laws are my joyous treasure forever. ¹¹² I am determined to obey You until I die.

¹¹³ I hate those who are undecided whether or not to obey You; but my choice is clear — I love Your law. ¹¹⁴ You are my refuge and my shield, and Your promises are my only source of hope. ¹¹⁵ Begone, you evil-minded men. Don't try to stop me from obeying God's commands. ¹¹⁶ Lord, You promised to let me live! Never let it be said that God failed me. ¹¹⁷ Hold me

safe above the heads of all my enemies; then I can
continue to obey Your laws.

[118] But You have rejected all who reject Your laws.
They are only fooling themselves. [119] The wicked are
the scum You skim off and throw away; no wonder I
love to obey Your laws! [120] I tremble in fear of You; I
fear Your punishments.

[121] Don't leave me to the mercy of my enemies, for
I have done what is right; I've been perfectly fair.
[122] Commit Yourself to bless me! Don't let the proud
oppress me! [123] My eyes grow dim with longing for
You to fulfill Your wonderful promise to rescue me.
[124] Lord, deal with me in lovingkindness, and teach
me, Your servant, to obey; [125] For I am Your servant;
therefore give me common sense to apply Your rules
to everything I do.

[126] Lord, it is time for You to act. For these evil
men have violated Your laws, [127] While I love Your
commandments more than the finest gold. [128] Every
law of God is right, whatever it concerns. I hate every
other way.

[129] Your laws are wonderful; no wonder I obey
them. [130] As Your plan unfolds, even the simple can
understand it. [131] No wonder I wait expectantly for
each of Your commands.

[132] Come and have mercy on me as is Your way
with those who love You. [133] Guide me with Your
laws so that I will not be overcome by evil. [134] Rescue
me from the oppression of evil men; then I can obey
You [135] Look down in love upon me and teach me all
Your laws. [136] I weep because Your laws are disobeyed.

137 O Lord, You are just and Your punishments are fair. 138 Your demands are just and right. 139 I am indignant and angry because of the way my enemies have disregarded Your laws. 140 I have thoroughly tested Your promises and that is why I love them so much. 141 I am worthless and despised, but I don't despise Your laws.

142 Your justice is eternal for Your laws are perfectly fair. 143 In my distress and anguish, Your commandments comfort me. 144 Your laws are always fair; help me to understand them and I shall live.

145 I am praying with great earnestness; answer me, O Lord, and I will obey Your laws. 146 "Save me," I cry, "for I am obeying." 147 Early in the morning, before the sun is up, I am praying and pointing out how much I trust in You. 148 I stay awake through the night to think about Your promises. 149 Because You are so loving and kind, listen to me and make me well again.

150 Here come these lawless men to attack me; 151 But You are near, O Lord; all Your commandments are based on truth. 152 I have known from earliest days that Your will never changes. 153 Look down upon my sorrows and rescue me, for I am obeying Your commands. 154 Yes, rescue me and give me back my life again just as You have promised. 155 The wicked are far from salvation for they do not care for Your laws. 156 Lord, how great is Your mercy: oh, give me back my life again.

157 My enemies are so many. They try to make me disobey; but I have not swerved from Your will. 158 I loathed these traitors because they care nothing for

Your laws. [159] Lord, see how much I really love Your demands. Now give me back my life and health because You are so kind. [160] There is utter truth in all Your laws; Your decrees are eternal.

[161] Great men have persecuted me, though they have no reason to, but I stand in awe of only Your words. [162] I rejoice in Your laws like one who finds a great treasure. [163] How I hate all falsehood but how I love Your laws. [164] I will praise You seven times a day because of Your wonderful laws.

[165] Those who love Your laws have great peace of heart and mind and do not stumble. [166] I long for Your salvation, Lord, and so I have obeyed Your laws. [167] I have looked for Your commandments and I love them very much; [168] Yes, I have searched for them. You know this because everything I do is known to You.

[169] O Lord, listen to my prayers; give me the common sense You promised. [170] Hear my prayers; rescue me as You said You would. [171] I praise You for letting me learn Your laws. [172] I will sing about their wonder, for each of them is just. [173] Stand ready to help me because I have chosen to follow Your will. [174] O Lord, I have longed for Your salvation and Your law is my delight. [175] If You will let me live, I will praise You; let Your laws assist me.

[176] I have wandered away like a lost sheep; come and find me for I have not turned away from Your commandments.

Proverbs for the Twenty-sixth Day

26 Honor doesn't go with fools any more than snow with summertime or rain with harvest time!

†

2 An undeserved curse has no effect. Its intended victim will be no more harmed by it than by a sparrow or swallow flitting through the sky.

†

3 Guide a horse with a whip, a donkey with a bridle, and a rebel with a rod to his back!

†

4, 5 When arguing with a rebel, don't use foolish arguments as he does, or you will become as foolish as he is! Prick his conceit with silly replies!

†

6 To trust a rebel to convey a message is as foolish as cutting off your feet and drinking poison!

†

7 In the mouth of a fool a proverb becomes as useless as a paralyzed leg.

†

8 Honoring a rebel will backfire like a stone tied to a slingshot!

⁹ A rebel will misapply an illustration so that its point will no more be felt than a thorn in the hand of a drunkard.

†

¹⁰ The master may get better work from an untrained apprentice than from a skilled rebel!

†

¹¹ As a dog returns to his vomit, so a fool repeats his folly.

†

¹² There is one thing worse than a fool, and that is a man who is conceited.

†

¹³ The lazy man won't go out and work. "There might be a lion outside!" he says.

†

¹⁴ He sticks to his bed like a door to its hinges!

†

¹⁵ He is too tired even to lift his food from his dish to his mouth!

†

¹⁶ Yet in his own opinion he is smarter than seven wise men.

†

¹⁷ Yanking a dog's ears is no more foolish than interfering in an argument that isn't any of your business.

†

¹⁸, ¹⁹ A man who is caught lying to his neighbor and says, "I was just fooling," is like a madman throwing around firebrands, arrows and death!

²⁰ Fire goes out for lack of fuel, and tensions disappear when gossip stops.

†

²¹ A quarrelsome man starts fights as easily as a match sets fire to paper.

†

²² Gossip is a dainty morsel eaten with great relish.

†

²³ Pretty words may hide a wicked heart, just as a pretty glaze covers a common clay pot.

†

²⁴⁻²⁶ A man with hate in his heart may sound pleasant enough, but don't believe him; for he is cursing you in his heart. Though he pretends to be so kind, his hatred will finally come to light for all to see.

†

²⁷ The man who sets a trap for others will get caught in it himself. Roll a boulder down on someone, and it will roll back and crush you.

†

²⁸ Flattery is a form of hatred and wounds cruelly.

Psalms for the Twenty-seventh Day

120 In my troubles I pled with God to help me and He did!

² Deliver me, O Lord, from liars. ³ O lying tongue, what shall be your fate? ⁴ You shall be pierced with sharp arrows and burned with glowing coals.

⁵, ⁶ My troubles pile high among these haters of the Lord, these men of Meshech and Kedar. I am tired of being here among these men who hate peace. ⁷ I am for peace, but they are for war, and my voice goes unheeded in their councils.

121 Shall I look to the mountain gods for help? ² No! My help is from Jehovah who made the mountains! And the heavens too! ³, ⁴ He will never let me stumble, slip or fall. For He is always watching, never sleeping.

⁵ Jehovah Himself is caring for you! He is your defender. ⁶ He protects you day and night. ⁷ He keeps you from all evil, and preserves your life. ⁸ He keeps His eye upon you as you come and go, and always guards you.

122 I was glad for the suggestion of going to Jerusalem, to the Temple of the Lord. ², ³ Now we are standing here inside the crowded city. ⁴ All Israel — Jehovah's people — have come to worship as the law requires, to thank and praise the Lord. ⁵ Look! There are the judges holding court beside the city gates, deciding all the people's arguments.

⁶ Pray for the peace of Jerusalem. May all who love this city prosper. ⁷ O Jerusalem, may there be peace within your walls and prosperity in your palaces. ⁸ This I ask for the sake of all my brothers and my friends who live here; ⁹ And may there be peace as a protection to the Temple of the Lord.

123 O God enthroned in heaven, I lift my eyes to You.

² We look to Jehovah our God for His mercy and kindness just as a servant keeps his eyes upon his master or a slave girl watches her mistress for the slightest signal.

^{3, 4} Have mercy on us, Lord, have mercy. For we have had our fill of contempt and of the scoffing of the rich and proud.

124 If the Lord had not been on our side (let all Israel admit it), if the Lord had not been on our side, ^{2, 3} We would have been swallowed alive by our enemies, destroyed by their anger. ^{4, 5} We would have drowned beneath the flood of these men's fury and pride.

⁶ Blessed be Jehovah who has not let them devour us. ⁷ We have escaped with our lives as a bird from a hunter's snare. The snare is broken and we are free!

⁸ Our help is from the Lord who made heaven and earth!

125 Those who trust in the Lord are steady as Mount Zion, unmoved by any circumstance.

² Just as the mountains surround and protect Jerusalem, so the Lord surrounds and protects His people.
³ For the wicked shall not rule the godly, lest the godly be forced to do wrong. ⁴ O Lord, do good to those who are good, whose hearts are right with the Lord; ⁵ But lead evil men to execution. And let Israel have quietness and peace.

126 When Jehovah brought back His exiles to Jerusalem, it was like a dream! ² How we laughed and sang for joy. And the other nations said, "What amazing things the Lord has done for them."

³ Yes, glorious things! What wonder! What joy!
⁴ May we be refreshed as by streams in the desert.

⁵ Those who sow tears shall reap joy. ⁶ Yes, they go out weeping, carrying seed for sowing and return singing, carrying their sheaves.

127 Unless the Lord builds a house, the builders' work is useless. Unless the Lord protects a city, sentries do no good. ² It is senseless for you to work so hard from early morning until late at night, fearing you will starve to death; for God wants His loved ones to get their proper rest.

³ Children are a gift from God; they are His reward.
⁴ Children born to a young man are like sharp arrows to defend him. ⁵ Happy is the man who has his quiver full of them. That man shall have the help he needs when arguing with his enemies.

128 Blessings on all who reverence and trust the Lord — on all who obey Him!

² Their reward shall be prosperity and happiness.
³ Your wife shall be contented in your home. And

look at all those children! There they sit around the
dinner table as vigorous and healthy as young olive
trees. ⁴ That is God's reward to those who reverence
and trust Him.

⁵ May the Lord continually bless you with heaven's
blessings as well as with human joys. ⁶ May you live
to enjoy your grandchildren! And may God bless
Israel!

129 Persecuted from my earliest youth (Israel is
speaking), ² And faced with never-ending discrimi-
nation — but not destroyed! My enemies have never
been able to finish me off! ³, ⁴ Though my back is
cut to ribbons with their whips, the Lord is good. For
He has snapped the chains that evil men had bound
me with.

⁵ May all who hate the Jews be brought to igno-
minious defeat. ⁶, ⁷ May they be as grass in shallow
soil, turning sear and yellow when half grown, ignored
by the reaper, despised by the binder. ⁸ And may
those passing by refuse to bless them by saying,
"Jehovah's blessings be upon you; we bless you in
Jehovah's name."

Proverbs for the Twenty-seventh Day

27 Don't brag about your plans for tomorrow —
wait and see what happens.

†

² Don't praise yourself; let others do it!

†

³ A rebel's frustrations are heavier than sand and
rocks.

†

⁴ Jealousy is more dangerous and cruel than anger.

†

⁵ Open rebuke is better than hidden love!

†

⁶ Wounds from a friend are better than kisses from
an enemy!

†

⁷ Even honey seems tasteless to a man who is full;
but if he is hungry, he'll eat anything!

†

⁸ A man who strays from home is like a bird that
wanders from its nest.

†

⁹ Friendly suggestions are as pleasant as perfume.

¹⁰ Never abandon a friend — either yours or your father's. Then you won't need to go to a distant relative for help in your time of need.

†

¹¹ My son, how happy I will be if you turn out to be sensible! It will be a public honor to me.

†

¹² A sensible man watches for problems ahead and prepares to meet them. The simpleton never looks, and suffers the consequences.

†

¹³ The world's poorest credit risk is the man who agrees to pay a stranger's debts.

†

¹⁴ If you shout a pleasant greeting to a friend too early in the morning, he will count it as a curse!

†

¹⁵ A constant dripping on a rainy day and a cranky woman are much alike! ¹⁶ You can no more stop her complaints than you can stop the wind or hold onto anything with oilslick hands.

†

¹⁷ A friendly discussion is as stimulating as the sparks that fly when iron strikes iron.

†

¹⁸ A workman may eat from the orchard he tends; anyone should be rewarded who protects another's interests.

†

¹⁹ A mirror reflects a man's face, but what he is really like is shown by the kind of friends he chooses.

†

²⁰ Ambition and death are alike in this: neither is ever satisfied.

²¹ The purity of silver and gold can be tested in a crucible, but a man is tested by his reaction to men's praise.

†

²² You can't separate a rebel from his foolishness though you crush him to powder.

†

²³, ²⁴ Riches can disappear fast. And the king's crown doesn't stay in his family forever — so watch your business interests closely. Know the state of your flocks and your herds; ²⁵, ²⁶, ²⁷ Then there will be lamb's wool enough for clothing, and goat's milk enough for food for all your household after the hay is harvested, and the new crop appears, and the mountain grasses are gathered in.

Psalms for the Twenty-eighth Day

130 O Lord, from the depths of despair I cry for Your help: ² "Hear me! Answer! Help me!"

³, ⁴ Lord, if You keep in mind our sins then who can ever get an answer to his prayers? But You forgive! What an awesome thing this is! ⁵ That is why I wait expectantly, trusting God to help, for He has promised. ⁶ I long for Him more than sentinels long for the dawn.

⁷ O Israel, hope in the Lord; for He is loving and kind, and comes to us with armloads of salvation. ⁸ He Himself shall ransom Israel from her slavery to sin.

131 Lord, I am not proud and haughty. I don't think myself better than others. I don't pretend to "know it all." ² I am quiet now before the Lord, just as a child who is weaned from the breast. Yes, my begging has been stilled.

³ O Israel, you too should quietly trust in the Lord — now, and always.

132 Lord, do You remember that time when my heart was so filled with turmoil? ², ³, ⁴, ⁵ I couldn't rest, I couldn't sleep, thinking how I ought to build a permanent home for the Ark of the Lord, a Temple for the mighty One of Israel. Then I vowed that I would do it; I made a solemn promise to the Lord.

⁶ First the Ark was in Ephrathah, then in the distant countryside of Jaar. ⁷ But now it will be settled in the Temple, in God's permanent home here on earth. That is where we will go to worship Him.

⁸ Arise, O Lord, and enter Your Temple with the Ark, the symbol of Your power. ⁹ We will clothe the priests in white, the symbol of all purity. May our nation shout for joy.

¹⁰ Do not reject Your servant David — the king You chose for Your people. ¹¹ For You promised me that my son would sit on my throne and succeed me. And surely You will never go back on a promise! ¹² You also promised that if my descendants will obey the terms of Your contract with me, then the dynasty of David shall never end.

¹³ O Lord, You have chosen Jerusalem as Your home: ¹⁴ "This is My permanent home where I shall live," You said, "for I have always wanted it this way. ¹⁵ I will make this city prosperous and satisfy her poor with food. ¹⁶ I will clothe her priests with salvation; her saints shall shout for joy. ¹⁷ David's power shall grow, for I have decreed for him a mighty Son. ¹⁸ I'll clothe His enemies with shame, but He shall be a glorious King."

133 How wonderful it is, how pleasant, when brothers live in harmony! ² For harmony is as precious as the fragrant anointing oil that was poured over Aaron's head, and ran down onto his beard, and onto the border of his robe. ³ Harmony is as refreshing as the dew on Mount Hermon, on the mountains of Israel. And God has pronounced this eternal blessing on Jerusalem, even life forevermore.

134 Oh, bless the Lord, you who serve Him as watchmen in the Temple every night. ² Lift your hands in holiness and bless the Lord

³ The Lord bless you from Zion — the Lord who made heaven and earth.

of Israel. And God has promised us his eternal bless-
the only salvation, even his one, no more

9:19 On those the Lord . . . you who serve him is . . .
workmen in the Temple . . . might . . . left ware . . .
chance, in darkness and bless the Lord . . .

The Lord bless you from Zion — the Lord who
made heaven and earth.

Proverbs for the Twenty-eighth Day

28 The wicked flee when no one is chasing them! But the godly are bold as lions!

†

² When there is moral rot within a nation, its government topples easily; but with honest, sensible leaders there is stability.

†

³ When a poor man oppresses those even poorer, he is like an unexpected flood sweeping away their last hope.

†

⁴ To complain about the law is to praise wickedness. To obey the law is to fight evil.

†

⁵ Evil men don't understand the importance of justice, but those who follow the Lord are much concerned about it.

†

⁶ Better to be poor and honest than rich and a cheater.

†

⁷ Young men who are wise obey the law; a son who is a member of a lawless gang is a shame to his father.

⁸ Income from exploiting the poor will end up in the hands of someone who pities them.

†

⁹ God doesn't listen to the prayers of men who flout the law.

†

¹⁰ A curse on those who lead astray the godly. But men who encourage the upright to do good shall be given a worthwhile reward.

†

¹¹ Rich men are conceited, but their real poverty is evident to the poor.

†

¹² When the godly are successful, everyone is glad. When the wicked succeed, everyone is sad.

†

¹³ A man who refuses to admit his mistakes can never be successful. But if he confesses and forsakes them, he gets another chance.

†

¹⁴ Blessed is the man who reveres God, but the man who doesn't care is headed for serious trouble.

†

¹⁵ A wicked ruler is as dangerous to the poor as a lion or bear attacking them.

†

¹⁶ Only a stupid prince will oppress his people, but a king will have a long reign if he hates dishonesty and bribes.

†

¹⁷ A murderer's conscience will drive him into hell. Don't stop him!

¹⁸ Good men will be rescued from harm, but cheaters will be destroyed.

†

¹⁹ Hard work brings prosperity; playing around brings poverty.

†

²⁰ The man who wants to do right will get a rich reward. But the man who wants to get rich quick will quickly fail.

†

²¹ Giving preferred treatment to rich people is a clear case of selling one's soul for a piece of bread.

†

²² Trying to get rich quick is evil and leads to poverty.

†

²³ In the end, people appreciate frankness more than flattery.

†

²⁴ A man who robs his parents and says, "What's wrong with that?" is no better than a murderer.

†

²⁵ Greed causes fighting; trusting God leads to prosperity.

†

²⁶ A man is a fool to trust himself! But those who use God's wisdom are safe.

†

²⁷ If you give to the poor, your needs will be supplied! But a curse upon those who close their eyes to poverty.

†

²⁸ When the wicked prosper, good men go away; when the wicked meet disaster, good men return.

Good men will be handed from harm, but the evil will be destroyed.

Hard work brings ... he wants; playing around brings poverty.

The man who wants to do right will get a rich reward. But the man who wants to get rich quick will quickly fail.

Doing ... pretend themselves to tell people to ... hungry ... soul has a piece of bread.

Doing to get rich quick, evil and leads to poverty.

In the end, people appreciate frankness more than flattery.

A man who robs his parents and says, "What's wrong with that?" is no better than a murderer.

Greed causes fighting; trusting God leads to prosperity.

A man is a fool to trust himself! But those who use God's wisdom are safe.

If you give to the poor, your needs will be supplied! But a curse upon those who close their eyes to poverty.

When the wicked prosper, good men go away; when the wicked meet disaster, good men return.

Psalms for the Twenty-ninth Day

135 Hallelujah! Yes, let His people praise Him, as they stand in His Temple courts. ³ Praise the Lord because He is so good; sing to His wonderful name. ⁴ For the Lord has chosen Israel as His personal possession.

⁵ I know the greatness of the Lord — that He is greater far than any other god. ⁶ He does whatever pleases Him throughout all of heaven and earth, and in the deepest seas. ⁷ He makes mists rise throughout the earth and sends the lightning to bring down the rain; and sends the winds from His treasuries. ⁸ He destroyed the eldest child in each Egyptian home, along with the firstborn of the flocks. ⁹ He did great miracles in Egypt before Pharaoh and all his people. ¹⁰ He smote great nations, slaying mighty kings — ¹¹ Sihon, king of Amorites; and Og, the king of Bashan; and the kings of Canaan — ¹² And gave their land as an eternal gift to His people Israel.

¹³ O Jehovah, Your name endures forever; Your fame is known to every generation. ¹⁴ For Jehovah will vindicate His people, and have compassion on His servants.

¹⁵ The heathen worship idols of gold and silver, made by men — ¹⁶ Idols with speechless mouths and

sightless eyes [17] And ears that cannot hear; they cannot even breathe. [18] Those who make them become like them! And so do all who trust in them!

[19] O Israel, bless Jehovah! High priests of Aaron, bless His name. [20] O Levite priests, bless the Lord Jehovah! Oh, bless His name, all of you who trust and reverence Him. [21] All people of Jerusalem, praise the Lord, for He lives here in Jerusalem. Hallelujah!

136 Oh, give thanks to the Lord, for He is good; His lovingkindness continues forever.

[2] Give thanks to the God of gods, for His lovingkindness continues forever. [3] Give thanks to the Lord of lords, for His lovingkindness continues forever. [4] Praise Him who alone does mighty miracles, for His lovingkindness continues forever. [5] Praise Him who made the heavens, for His lovingkindness continues forever. [6] Praise Him who planted the water within the earth, for His lovingkindness continues forever. [7] Praise Him who made the heavenly lights, for His lovingkindness continues forever: [8] The sun to rule the day, for His lovingkindness continues forever; [9] And the moon and stars at night, for His lovingkindness continues forever. [10] Praise the God who smote the firstborn of Egypt, for His lovingkindness to Israel continues forever. [11, 12] He brought them out with mighty power and upraised fist to strike their enemies, for His lovingkindness to Israel continues forever. [13] Praise the Lord who opened the Red Sea to make a path before them, for His lovingkindness continues forever, [14] And led them safely through, for His lovingkindness continues forever — [15] But drowned Pharaoh's army in the sea, for His lovingkindness to Israel continues forever.

¹⁶ Praise Him who led His people through the wilderness for His lovingkindness continues forever. ¹⁷ Praise Him who saved His people from the power of mighty kings, for His lovingkindness continues forever, ¹⁸ And killed famous kings who were their enemies, for His lovingkindness to Israel continues forever: ¹⁹ Sihon, king of Amorites — for God's lovingkindness to Israel continues forever — ²⁰ And Og, king of Bashan — for His lovingkindness to Israel continues forever. ²¹ God gave the land of these kings to Israel as a gift forever, for His lovingkindness to Israel continues forever; ²² Yes, a permanent gift to His servant Israel, for His lovingkindness continues forever.

²³ He remembered our utter weakness, for His lovingkindness continues forever. ²⁴ And saved us from our foes, for His lovingkindness continues forever.

²⁵ He gives food to every living thing, for His lovingkindness continues forever. ²⁶ Oh, give thanks to the God of heaven, for His lovingkindness continues forever.

137 Weeping, we sat beside the rivers of Babylon thinking of Jerusalem. ² We have put away our lyres, hanging them upon the branches of the willow trees, ³, ⁴ For how can we sing? Yet our captors, our tormentors, demand that we sing for them the happy songs of Zion! ⁵, ⁶ If I forget you, O Jerusalem, let my right hand forget her skill upon the harp. If I fail to love her more than my highest joy, let me never sing again.

⁷ O Jehovah, do not forget what these Edomites did on that day when the armies of Babylon captured Jerusalem. "Raze her to the ground!" they yelled.

⁸ O Babylon, evil beast, you shall be destroyed. Blessed is the man who destroys you as you have destroyed us. ⁹ Blessed is the man who takes your babies and smashes them against the rocks!

138 Lord, with all my heart I thank You. I will sing Your praises before the armies of angels in heaven. ² I face Your Temple as I worship, giving thanks to You for all Your lovingkindness and Your faithfulness, for Your promises are backed by all the honor of Your name. ³ When I pray, You answer me, and encourage me by giving me the strength I need.

⁴ Every king in all the earth shall give You thanks, O Lord, for all of them shall hear Your voice. ⁵ Yes, they shall sing about Jehovah's glorious ways, for His glory is very great. ⁶ Yet though He is so great, He respects the humble; but proud men must keep their distance. ⁷ Though I am surrounded by troubles, You will bring me safely through them. You will clench Your fist against my angry enemies! Your power will save me. ⁸ The Lord will work out His plans for my life — for Your lovingkindness, Lord, continues forever. Don't abandon me — for You made me.

139 O Lord, You have examined my heart and know everything about me. ² You know when I sit or stand. When far away You know my every thought. ³ You chart the path ahead of me, and tell me where to stop and rest! Every moment, You know where I am! ⁴ You know what I am going to say before I even say it. ⁵ You both precede and follow me, and place Your hand of blessing on my head.

⁶ This is too glorious, too wonderful to believe! ⁷ I can *never* be lost to Your Spirit. I can *never* get

away from God! ⁸ If I go up to heaven You are there;
if I go down to the place of the dead, You are there.
⁹ If I ride the morning winds to the farthest oceans,
¹⁰ Even there Your hand will guide me, Your strength
will support me. ¹¹ If I try to hide in the darkness,
the night becomes light around me! ¹² For even darkness cannot hide from God; to You the night shines
as bright as day. Darkness and light are both alike
to You.

¹³ You made all the delicate, inner parts of my
body, and knit them together in my mother's womb.
¹⁴ Thank You for making me so wonderfully complex!
It is amazing to think about. Your workmanship is
marvelous — and how well I know it. ¹⁵ You were
there while I was being formed in utter seclusion!
¹⁶ You saw me before I was born and scheduled each
day of my life before I began to breathe. Every day
was recorded in Your Book!

¹⁷, ¹⁸ How precious it is, Lord, to realize that You
are thinking about me constantly! I can't even count
how many times a day Your thoughts turn towards
me! And when I waken in the morning, You are still
thinking of me!

¹⁹ Surely You will slay the wicked, Lord! Away,
bloodthirsty men! Begone! ²⁰ They blaspheme Your
name and stand in arrogance against You — how silly
can they be? ²¹ O Lord, shouldn't I hate those who
hate You? Shouldn't I be grieved with them? ²² Yes,
I hate them, for Your enemies are my enemies too.

²³ Search me, O God, and know my heart, test my
thoughts. ²⁴ Point out anything You find in me that
makes You sad, and lead me along the path of everlasting life.

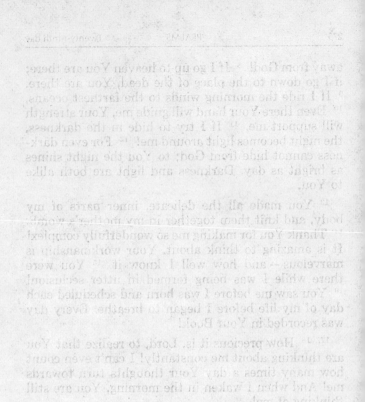

Proverbs for the Twenty-ninth Day

29 The man who is often reproved but refuses to accept criticism will suddenly be broken and never have another chance.

†

² With good men in authority, the people rejoice; but with the wicked in power, they groan.

†

³ A wise son makes his father happy, but a lad who hangs around with prostitutes disgraces him.

†

⁴ A just king gives stability to his nation, but one who demands bribes destroys it.

†

⁵, ⁶ Flattery is a trap; evil men are caught in it, but good men stay away and sing for joy.

†

⁷ The good man knows the poor man's rights; the godless don't care.

†

⁸ Fools start fights everywhere while wise men try to keep peace.

†

⁹ There's no use arguing with a fool. He only rages and scoffs, and tempers flare.

¹⁰ The godly pray for those who long to kill them.

†

¹¹ A rebel shouts in anger; a wise man holds his temper in and cools it.

†

¹² A wicked ruler will have wicked aides on his staff.

†

¹³ Rich and poor are alike in this: each depends on God for light.

†

¹⁴ A king who is fair to the poor shall have a long reign.

†

¹⁵ Scolding and spanking a child helps him to learn. Left to himself, he brings shame to his mother.

†

¹⁶ When rulers are wicked, their people are too; but good men will live to see the tyrant's downfall.

†

¹⁷ Discipline your son and he will give you happiness and peace of mind.

†

¹⁸ Where there is ignorance of God, the people run wild; but what a wonderful thing it is for a nation to know and keep His laws!

†

¹⁹ Sometimes mere words are not enough — discipline is needed. For the words may not be heeded.

†

²⁰ There is more hope for a fool than for a man of quick temper.

²¹ Pamper a servant from childhood, and he will expect you to treat him as a son!

†

²² A hot-tempered man starts fights and gets into all kinds of trouble.

†

²³ Pride ends in a fall, while humility brings honor.

†

²⁴ A man who assists a thief must really hate himself! For he knows the consequence but does it anyway.

†

²⁵ Fear of man is a dangerous trap, but to trust in God means safety.

†

²⁶ Do you want justice? Don't fawn on the judge, but ask the Lord for it!

†

²⁷ The good hate the badness of the wicked. The wicked hate the goodness of the good.

²¹ Pamper a servant from childhood and he will expect you to treat him as a son.

†

²² A hot-tempered man starts fights and gets into all kinds of trouble.

†

²³ Pride ends in a fall, while humility brings honor.

†

²⁴ A man who assists a thief must really hate himself. For he knows the consequence but does it anyway.

†

²⁵ Fear of man is a dangerous trap, but to trust in God means safety.

†

²⁶ Do you want justice? Don't fawn on the judge, but ask the Lord for it!

†

²⁷ The good hate the badness of the wicked. The wicked hate the goodness of the good.

Psalms for the Thirtieth Day

140 O Lord, deliver me from evil men. Preserve me from the violent, ² Who plot and stir up trouble all day long. ³ Their words sting like poisonous snakes. ⁴ Keep me out of their power. Preserve me from their violence, for they are plotting against me. ⁵ These proud men have set a trap to catch me, a noose to yank me up and leave me dangling in the air; they wait in ambush with a net to throw over and hold me helpless in its meshes.

⁶, ⁷, ⁸ O Jehovah, my Lord and Savior, my God and my shield — hear me as I pray! Don't let these wicked men succeed; don't let them prosper and be proud. ⁹ Let their plots boomerang! Let them be destroyed by the very evil they have planned for me. ¹⁰ Let burning coals fall down upon their heads, or throw them into the fire, or into deep pits from which they can't escape.

¹¹ Don't let liars prosper here in our land; quickly punish them. ¹² But the Lord will surely help those they persecute; He will maintain the rights of the poor. ¹³ Surely the godly are thanking You, for they shall live in Your presence.

141 Quick, Lord, answer me — for I have prayed. Listen when I cry to You for help! ² Regard my prayer as my evening sacrifice and as incense wafting up to You.

³ Help me, Lord, to keep my mouth shut and my lips sealed. ⁴ Take away my lust for evil things; don't let me want to be with sinners, doing what they do, sharing their dainties. ⁵ Let the godly smite me! It will be a kindness! If they reprove me, it is medicine! Don't let me refuse it. But I am in constant prayer against the wicked and their deeds. ⁶, ⁷ When their leaders are condemned, and their bones are strewn across the ground, then these men will finally listen to me and know that I am trying to help them.

⁸ I look to You for help, O Lord God. You are my refuge. Don't let them slay me. ⁹ Keep me out of their traps. ¹⁰ Let them fall into their own snares, while I escape.

142 How I plead with God, how I implore His mercy, pouring out my troubles before Him. ³ For I am overwhelmed and desperate, and You alone know which way I ought to turn to miss the traps my enemies have set for me. ⁴ (There's one — just over there to the right!) No one gives me a passing thought. No one will help me; no one cares one whit what happens to me. ⁵ Then I prayed to Jehovah. "Lord," I pled, "You are my only place of refuge. Only You can keep me safe.

⁶ Hear my cry, for I am very low. Rescue me from my persecutors, for they are too strong for me. ⁷ Bring me out of prison, so that I can thank You. The godly will rejoice with me for all Your help."

143 Hear my prayer, O Lord; answer my plea, because You are faithful to Your promises. ² Don't bring me to trial! For as compared with You, no one is perfect.

³ My enemies chased and caught me. They have knocked me to the ground. They force me to live in the darkness like those in the grave. ⁴ I am losing all hope; I am paralyzed with fear.

⁵ I remember the glorious miracles You did in days of long ago. ⁶ I reach out for You. I thirst for You as parched land thirsts for rain. ⁷ Come quickly, Lord, and answer me, for my depression deepens; don't turn away from me or I shall die. ⁸ Let me see Your kindness to me in the morning, for I am trusting You. Show me where to walk, for my prayer is sincere. ⁹ Save me from my enemies, O Lord, I run to You to hide me. ¹⁰ Help me to do Your will, for You are my God. Lead me in good paths, for Your Spirit is good.

¹¹ Lord, saving me will bring glory to Your name. Bring me out of all this trouble because You are true to Your promises. ¹² And because You are loving and kind to me, cut off all my enemies and destroy those who are trying to harm me; for I am Your servant.

144 Bless the Lord who is my immovable Rock. He gives me strength and skill in battle. ² He is always kind and loving to me; He is my fortress, my tower of strength and safety, my deliverer. He stands before me as a shield. He subdues my people under me.

³ O Lord, what is man that You even notice him? Why bother at all with the human race? ⁴ For man is but a breath; his days are like a passing shadow.

⁵ Bend down the heavens, Lord, and come. The mountains smoke beneath Your touch. ⁶ Let loose

Your lightning bolts, Your arrows, Lord, upon Your enemies, and scatter them. ⁷ Reach down from heaven and rescue me; deliver me from deep waters, from the power of my enemies. ⁸ Their mouths are filled with lies; they swear to the truth of what is false.

⁹ I will sing You a new song, O God, with a ten-stringed harp. ¹⁰ For You grant victory to kings! You are the one who will rescue Your servant David from the fatal sword. ¹¹ Save me! Deliver me from these enemies, these liars, these treacherous men.

¹²⁻¹⁵ Here is my description of a truly happy land where Jehovah is God:

Sons vigorous and tall as growing plants.

Daughters of graceful beauty like the pillars of a palace wall.

Barns full to the brim with crops of every kind.

Sheep by the thousands out in our fields.

Oxen loaded down with produce.

No enemy attacking the walls, but peace everywhere.

No crime in our streets.

Yes, happy are those whose God is Jehovah.

Proverbs for the Thirtieth Day

30 *These are the messages of Agur, son of Jakeh, from Massa, addressed to Ithiel and Ucal:*

✝

² I am tired out, O God, and ready to die. I am too stupid even to call myself a human being! ³ I cannot understand man, let alone God. ⁴ Who else but God goes back and forth to heaven? Who else holds the wind in His fists, and wraps up the oceans in His cloak? Who but God has created the world? If there is any other, what is his name — and his son's name — if you know it?

✝

⁵ Every word of God proves true. He defends all who come to Him for protection. ⁶ Do not add to His words, lest He rebuke you, and you be found a liar.

✝

⁷ O God, I beg two favors from you before I die: ⁸ First, help me never to tell a lie. Second, give me neither poverty nor riches! Give me just enough to satisfy my needs! ⁹ For if I grow rich, I may become content without God. And if I am too poor, I may steal, and thus insult God's holy name. ¹⁰ Never falsely accuse a man to his employer, lest he curse you for your sin.

11, 12 There are those who curse their father and mother, and feel themselves faultless despite their many sins. 13, 14 They are proud beyond description, arrogant, disdainful. They devour the poor with teeth as sharp as knives!

†

15 There are two things never satisfied, like a leech forever craving more: no, three things! no, four!

16 Hell
   The barren womb
   A barren desert
   Fire

†

17 A man who mocks his father and despises his mother shall have his eye plucked out by ravens and eaten by vultures.

†

18 There are three things too wonderful for me to understand — no, four!

19 How an eagle glides through the sky.
   How a serpent crawls upon a rock.
   How a ship finds its way across the heaving ocean.
   The growth of love between a man and a girl.

†

20 There is another thing too: how a prostitute can sin and then say, "What's wrong with that?"

†

21 There are three things that make the earth tremble — no, four it cannot stand:

22, 23 A slave who becomes a king.
   A rebel who prospers.
   A bitter woman when she finally marries.
   A servant girl who marries her mistress' husband.

24, 25, 26, 27, 28 There are four things that are small but unusually wise:

> Ants: they aren't strong, but store up food for the winter.
>
> Cliff badgers: delicate little animals who protect themselves by living among the rocks.
>
> The locusts: though they have no leader, they stay together in swarms.
>
> The spiders: they are easy to catch and kill, yet are found even in king's palaces!

†

29 There are three stately monarchs in the earth — no, four:

> 30, 31 The lion, king of the animals. He won't turn aside for anyone.
>
> The peacock.
>
> The he-goat.
>
> A king as he leads his army.

†

32 If you have been a fool by being proud or plotting evil, don't brag about it — cover your mouth with your hand in shame.

†

33 As the churning of cream yields butter, and a blow to the nose causes bleeding, so anger causes quarrels.

Psalms for the Thirty-first Day

145 I will praise You, my God and King, and bless Your name each day and forever.

³ Great is Jehovah! Greatly praise Him! His greatness is beyond discovery! ⁴ Let each generation tell its children what glorious things He does. ⁵ I will meditate about Your glory, splendor, majesty and miracles. ⁶ Your awe-inspiring deeds shall be on every tongue; I will proclaim Your greatness. ⁷ Everyone will tell about how good You are, and sing about Your righteousness.

⁸ Jehovah is kind and merciful, slow to get angry, full of love. ⁹ He is good to everyone, and His compassion is intertwined with everything He does. ¹⁰ All living things shall thank You, Lord, and Your people will bless You. ¹¹ They will talk together about the glory of Your kingdom and mention examples of Your power. ¹² They will tell about Your miracles and about the majesty and glory of Your reign. ¹³ For Your kingdom never ends. You rule generation after generation.

¹⁴ The Lord lifts the fallen and those bent beneath their loads. ¹⁵ The eyes of all mankind look up to You for help; You give them their food as they need it. ¹⁶ You constantly satisfy the hunger and thirst of every living thing.

¹⁷ The Lord is fair in everything He does, and full of kindness. ¹⁸ He is close to all who call on Him sincerely. ¹⁹ He fulfills the desires of those who reverence and trust Him; He hears their cries for help and rescues them. ²⁰ He protects all those who love Him, but destroys the wicked.

²¹ I shall praise the Lord and call on all men everywhere to bless His holy name forever and forever.

146 Praise the Lord! Yes, really praise Him! ² I will praise Him as long as I live, yes, even with my dying breath.

³ Don't look to men for help; their greatest leaders fail; ⁴ For every man must die. His breathing stops, life ends, and in a moment all he planned for himself is ended. ⁵ But happy is the man who has the God of Jacob as his helper, whose hope is in the Lord his God — ⁶ The God who made both heaven and earth, the seas and everything in them. He is the God who keeps every promise, ⁷ And gives justice to the poor and oppressed, and food to the hungry. He frees the prisoners, ⁸ And opens the eyes of the blind; He lifts the burdens from those bent down beneath their loads. For the Lord loves good men. ⁹ He protects the immigrants, and cares for the orphans and widows. But He turns topsy-turvy the plans of the wicked.

¹⁰ The Lord will reign forever. O Jerusalem, your God is King in every generation! Hallelujah! Praise the Lord!

147 Hallelujah! Yes, praise the Lord! How good it is to sing His praises! How delightful, and how right!

² He is rebuilding Jerusalem and bringing back the exiles. ³ He heals the broken-hearted, binding up

their wounds. ⁴ He counts the stars and calls them all by name. ⁵ How great He is! His power is absolute! His understanding is unlimited. ⁶ The Lord supports the humble, but brings the wicked into the dust. ⁷ Sing out your thanks to Him; sing praises to our God, accompanied by harps. ⁸ He covers the heavens with clouds, sends down the showers and makes the green grass grow in mountain pastures. ⁹ He feeds the wild animals and the young ravens cry to Him for food. ¹⁰ The speed of a horse is nothing to Him. How puny in His sight is the strength of a man. ¹¹ But His joy is in those who reverence Him; those who expect Him to be loving and kind.

¹² Praise Him, O Jerusalem! Praise Your God, O Zion! ¹³ For He has fortified your gates against all enemies, and blessed your children. ¹⁴ He sends peace across your nation, and fills your barns with plenty of the finest wheat. ¹⁵ He sends His orders to the world. How swiftly His Word flies. ¹⁶ He sends the snow in all its lovely whiteness, and scatters the frost upon the ground, ¹⁷ And hurls the hail upon the earth. Who can stand before His freezing cold? ¹⁸ But then He calls for warmer weather, and the spring winds blow and all the river ice is broken. ¹⁹ He has made known His laws and ceremonies of worship to Israel — ²⁰ Something He has not done with any other nation; they have not known His commands.

Hallelujah! Yes, praise the Lord!

148 Praise the Lord, O heavens! Praise Him from the skies! ² Praise Him, all His angels, all the armies of heaven. ³ Praise Him sun and moon, and all you twinkling stars. ⁴ Praise Him, skies above. Praise Him, vapors high above the clouds.

⁵ Let everything He has made give praise to Him! For He issued His command, and they came into being; ⁶ He established them forever and forever. His orders will never be revoked.

⁷ And praise Him down here on earth, you creatures of the ocean depths. ⁸ Let fire and hail, snow, rain, wind and weather, all obey. ⁹ Let the mountains and hills, the fruit trees and cedars, ¹⁰ The wild animals and cattle, the snakes and birds, ¹¹ The kings and all the people, with their rulers and their judges, ¹² Young men and maidens, old men and children — ¹³ All praise the Lord together. For He alone is worthy. His glory is far greater than all of earth and heaven. ¹⁴ He has made His people strong, honoring His godly ones — the people of Israel, the people closest to Him.

Hallelujah! Yes, praise the Lord!

149 Hallelujah! Yes, praise the Lord! Sing Him a new song. Sing His praises, all His people.

² O Israel, rejoice in your Maker. O people of Jerusalem, exult in Your King. ³ Praise His name by marching together to the Temple, accompanied by drums and lyre.

⁴, ⁵ For Jehovah enjoys His people; He will save the humble. Let His people rejoice in this honor. Let them sing for joy as they lie upon their beds. ⁶, ⁷ Adore Him, O His people! And take a double-edged sword to execute His punishment upon the nations. ⁸ Bind their kings and leaders with iron chains, ⁹ And execute their sentences.

He is the glory of His people. Hallelujah! Praise Him!

150 Hallelujah! Yes, praise the Lord!

Praise Him in His Temple, and in the heavens He made with mighty power. ² Praise Him for His mighty works. Praise His unequaled greatness. ³ Praise Him with the trumpet and with lute and harp. ⁴ Praise Him with the timbrels and processional. Praise Him with stringed instruments and horns. ⁵ Praise Him with cymbals, yes, loud clanging cymbals.

⁶ Let everything alive give praises to the Lord! *You* praise Him!

Hallelujah!

150) Hallelujah! You praise the Lord.

Praise Him in His Temple, and in the heavens He made with mighty power. Praise Him for His mighty works. Praise His unequaled greatness. Praise Him with the trumpet and with lyre and harp. Praise Him with the timbrel and praise Him. Praise Him with stringed instruments and horns. Praise Him with cymbals, yes, loud clashing cymbals.

Let everything alive give praise to the Lord! You praise Him.

Hallelujah.

Proverbs for the Thirty-first Day

31 *These are the wise sayings of King Lemuel of Massa, taught to him at his mother's knee:*

†

² O my son, whom I have dedicated to the Lord,
³ Do not spend your time with women — the royal pathway to destruction.

†

⁴And it is not for kings, O Lemuel, to drink wine and whiskey. ⁵ For if they drink they may forget their duties and be unable to give justice to those who are oppressed. ⁶, ⁷ Hard liquor is for sick men at the brink of death, and wine for those in deep depression. Let them drink to forget their poverty and misery.

†

⁸ You should defend those who cannot help themselves. ⁹ Yes, speak up for the poor and needy and see that they get justice.

†

¹⁰ If you can find a truly good wife, she is worth more than precious gems! ¹¹ Her husband can trust her, and she will richly satisfy his needs. ¹² She will not hinder him, but help him all her life. ¹³ She finds wool and flax and busily spins it. ¹⁴ She buys imported foods, brought by ship from distant ports.

¹⁵ She gets up before dawn to prepare breakfast for her household, and plans the day's work for her servant girls. ¹⁶ She goes out to inspect a field, and buys it; with her own hands she plants a vineyard. ¹⁷ She is energetic, a hard worker, ¹⁸ And watches for bargains. She works far into the night!

†

¹⁹, ²⁰ She sews for the poor, and generously gives to the needy. ²¹ She has no fear of winter for her household, for she has made warm clothes for all of them. ²² She also upholsters with finest tapestry; her own clothing is beautifully made — a purple gown of pure linen. ²³ Her husband is well known, for he sits in the council chamber with the other civic leaders. ²⁴ She makes belted linen garments to sell to the merchants.

†

²⁵ She is a woman of strength and dignity, and has no fear of old age. ²⁶ When she speaks, her words are wise, and kindness is the rule for everything she says. ²⁷ She watches carefully all that goes on throughout her household, and is never lazy. ²⁸ Her children stand and bless her; so does her husband. He praises her with these words: ²⁹ "There are many fine women in the world, but you are the best of them all!"

†

³⁰ Charm can be deceptive and beauty doesn't last, but a woman who fears and reverences God shall be greatly praised. ³¹ Praise her for the many fine things she does. These good deeds of hers shall bring her honor and recognition from even the leaders of the nation.

INTERPRETIVE NOTE

PSALMS

When the eleven disciples gathered in the Upper Room on the night of Christ's resurrection, we are told that they were greatly disturbed and fearful. Then the Lord entered the room and said to them, "Peace." What He brought to the disciples He can bring to the mind and heart of any individual who will let Him in.

He began His discourse to the disciples by saying, "Peace be unto you . . . Behold my hands and my feet that it is I, myself. Handle me and see, for a spirit hath not flesh and bones as ye see me have." Then He turned to them and said, "Have ye any meat?" He concluded, "These are the words which I spake unto you while I was yet with you, that all things must be fulfilled, which were written in the Law of Moses, and in the prophets and in the Psalms concerning me." And Luke adds: "Then opened he their understanding, that they might understand the Scriptures."

Thus it is on the authority of the Lord Jesus Christ Himself that we are to find Christ in the Psalms. No one can properly understand the Cross, or fathom why He endured its agony, without having studied the Psalms. For example, when we read Luke 24 we see its relationship to Psalm 1. The first three verses of Psalm 1 convey that the man who does not follow the advice of evil men is blessed and happy.

"Oh, the joys of those who do not follow evil men's advice . . . scoffing at the things of God: but they delight in doing everything God wants them to, and day and night are always meditating on His laws . . . They are like trees along a river bank bearing luscious fruit each season without fail. Their leaves shall never wither, and all they do shall prosper."

The only one who ever could experience this completely is the Lord Jesus Christ, for He is the only one who never walked in the counsel of the ungodly.

While the first three verses of Psalm 1 speak particularly of Christ, yet the one who believes in Christ can also describe his position with the Lord in terms of these verses. Certainly there is no true and lasting happiness in this world today apart from the Blessed One, that is to say, apart from the Lord Jesus Christ.

† † †

PROVERBS

Of all the inspired thoughts in the book of Proverbs, the key statement is found in chapter three, verse 13: "The man who knows right from wrong and has good judgment and common sense is happier than the man who is immensely rich." When we read God's Word it is God speaking to man. When the Christian prays, it is man speaking to God.

In the Psalms the Christian is found on his knees. In the book of Proverbs the Christian is on his feet doing things. The Psalms are for devotion; the Proverbs are for the Christian's walk and warfare. The Proverbs are for the businessman, the layman, the housewife, and the young person in his everyday walk and life, as well as for the church leader.

In the opening verse we read the superscription, "These are the proverbs of King Solomon of Israel, David's son." We are told that what follows is given for our wisdom and instruction. Solomon was a great scientist and philosopher. He was also architect of one of the wonders of the ancient world, the temple at Jerusalem. He was also a king. In 1 Kings 4:29, 31-32, KJV, we read that God had given him "wisdom and understanding exceeding much, and largeness of heart even as the sand that is on the seashore."

Solomon gathered these sayings given by the Holy Spirit, arranged them in an orderly fashion, and preserved them for us and our daily instruction.

In the first ten chapters of Proverbs we find counsel for young people. The second ten provide counsel for all men everywhere. The next chapters, 21-30, are counsel for kings and rulers, and the book closes with chapter 31, a beautiful description of women's rights.

May you find much joy and strength in your reading, and may you find, as Solomon did, that "Timely advice is as lovely as golden apples in a silver basket." (Proverbs 25:11).

G. M. W.

WHERE TO FIND HELP
in the Psalms

Read these chapters when you . . .

Feel troubled 17, 20, 23, 27, 28, 40, 43, 54, 57, 61, 62, 63, 64, 86

Feel persecuted 56, 59, 69, 70, 102, 140, 141, 142, 143

Feel "cornered" 36, 68

Feel things have "gone sour" 42

Feel like complaining 39

Feel envious of people 73

Feel your friends have turned against you 35, 41, 55

Need assurance 3

Are angry with someone 133

Have sinned 32, 51, 79, 80, 106, 130

Need help 38, 83

Are facing important decisions 25, 26, 91

Are troubled by Godlessness in the world 2, 9, 46, 52, 75, 76

Need encouragement as a senior citizen 71

Feel timid about sharing your faith 67

Have responsibility in governing others 21, 72, 82, 94

Find it difficult to be thankful 66

To get your mind off yourself, praise God 92, 96, 97, 98, 100, 117, 136, 138, 139, 145, 147, 148, 150

THESE PSALMS
will remind you that:

God and one are a majority 18

God is worth trusting 4, 29, 33, 34, 65, 99, 118

God loves His own 8, 31, 81, 91, 105, 106, 111, 121, 149

God hears our prayers 103, 108, 116

God is alive 8, 14, 84, 115

God is in control of history 24, 45, 47, 87, 99, 110, 124, 135

God is incomparable 19, 65, 107, 113, 114, 146

God is the source of life 104

God's words are most important 119

Godly living is great living 1, 15, 16, 112, 127, 128

Godly living benefits a nation 78, 144

Our Creator can best guide our lives 25, 37

Those who govern should honor God 21

We should pray for the Jews 44, 48, 74, 122, 126, 129, 132

Jesus suffered, too 22

We should keep our perspective in life 90, 93

No one fools God 5, 10, 11, 12, 50, 53

Man alone is nothing 2, 9, 49, 124, 131

We are sinful 32

HIGHLIGHTS IN PROVERBS
on the subjects of:

Business (see also "success")   14:4; 16:11; 24:3, 4, 27; 25:13; 27:23-27

Children, raising of   13:24; 14:26; 19:18; 22:6; 23:13, 14; 29:15, 17

Communicating   1:1-3; 13:17; 16:23; 24:26; 27:9

Counsel   10:20, 21, 31; 12:1, 15, 26; 13:1, 10, 14, 18; 14:7, 15; 15:5, 7, 23, 31, 32; 18:2, 13, 15, 20; 19:2, 20; 20:5, 18; 23:12, 23; 25:11; 28:13; 29:1

Friendliness   12:25; 16:28; 17:9, 17; 18:24; 27:10, 19

Goals in life   3:21-26

Government   8:14-16; 11:14; 14:35; 16:10, 12; 17:23; 18:5; 20:8, 26, 28; 22:8; 28:2, 15, 16; 29:2, 4, 12, 14, 16

Health   3:7, 8; 4:21, 22; 14:27, 30; 15:4, 15, 30; 16:24; 17:22; 19:23

Immorality   2:16-19; 4:23-27; chap. 5; 6:24-35; chap. 7; 9:13-18; 22:14; 23:26-28; 24:8; 30:20

Integrity   3:27, 28; 11:1, 3, 6; 12:13, 17, 22; 13:5; 14:25; 15:3; 16:2, 11; 17:15; 19:5, 9, 28; 20:10, 21, 23; 21:2, 3; 22:1; 30:10

Justice   3:33; 10:30; 11:19, 21, 31; 12:7, 19; 13:23; 14:11, 19, 32; 29:17, 22; 22:7, 18; 24:11, 12, 19, 20; 28:5; 29:26

Key to life   3:4-8; 8:13; 22:17-19

Liquor   20:1; 23:19-20, 29-35; 31:4-7

Marriage   11:29; 12:4; 14:1; 18:22; 19:14; 21:9, 19; 27:15, 16; 31:10-31

Money-lending   6:1-5; 11:15; 17:18; 20:16; 22:26-27; 27:13